D1542828

Who's Afraid of Edward Albee?
by Foster Hirsch

NUMBER FOUR
MODERN AUTHORS MONOGRAPH SERIES

Creative Arts Book Company
Berkeley • 1978

This project is supported in part by a grant
from The National Endowment for the Arts in
Washington, D.C., a Federal Agency.

Published by Creative Arts Book Company,
833 Bancroft Way, Berkeley, CA 94710.

ISBN 0-916870-12-X
Library of Congress Card Catalog #78-52773

Cover Design by Paula Gill

Contents

I

Delicate Balances

At the end of Edward Albee's most famous play, George asks Martha the question that the audience has been waiting to hear: "Who's afraid of Virginia Woolf?" "I am, George, I am," she whispers, drained, yielding. She's admitting, finally, that she is afraid of reality—of a world without the comfort of the imaginary child she and George have created as both a denial and reminder of their barren marriage.

Like Martha, most of Albee's characters are afraid of the world out there. In play after play, characters are haunted by the recurrent fear that beneath the ordered appearances of their lives there might really be nothing there, that living amounts merely to so many desperate maneuvers to cover a vacuum. And bearing down on the characters is the spectre of their own mortality. From Grandma, preparing for her end in the early one-acts, *The American Dream* and *The Sandbox,* to a young girl taking her own life in *Listening,* his most recent drama, Albee's work is obsessed with deaths both real and symbolic. Vulnerable to reality, their lives delicately balanced between order and chaos, all of Albee's characters are afraid of "Virginia Woolf."

Albee made his mark early. His one-acts, and *Who's Afraid of Virginia Woolf?,* his first full-length piece, established him as a major playwright. Critics labeled him as a kind of Peck's Bad Boy among American dramatists—the native counterpart to England's Angry Young Men, the most vigorous, tough-minded, and promising of a new breed of writers for the theatre. In *Fam and Yam,* a novice one-act, Albee constructs a fictitious interview between Yam, a hip young playwright on the make, and Fam, a famous old-guard playwright. Both writers are satirized, Yam for spouting radical theatre cliches, Fam for being so smugly commercial. Albee himself, in the nearly twenty years that he has been writing, has never become a slick traditional writer turning out cut-rate commodities for the popular Broadway audience. But he has not, on the other hand, entirely fulfilled his promise as the fierce, iconoclastic avant-garde stylist, ripping through the fabric of the American Dream. His early work is gaudy and audacious. Since *A Delicate Balance* (1966), his wisest play but one which introduced a more sober and measured tone to his writing, Albee's dramas have become increasingly rarefied. As his themes, his characters, and his language have become more abstract, his plays have declined in relevance and dramatic interest. Like many of the characters, Albee himself has seemed increasingly unwilling to face up to "Virginia Woolf." Albee, the angry young writer, has become a middle-aged ascetic, fashioning meticulously scored poetic dramas on abstract themes.

The question to ask now, at this diminished moment in the career of an enormously gifted writer, is "Who's afraid of Edward Albee?"; and the answer, on the evidence of his progressively claustrophobic and indirect plays, from which his own biography is carefully omitted, is—Albee himself.

A history professor and his wife invent an imaginary child. An upper-middle-class suburban couple is visited by their best friends, who bring with them a mysterious plague. A husband and wife, on vacation at the seashore, encounter talking sea creatures. These skeletal outlines of three representative plays (*Who's Afraid of Virginia Woolf?*, *A Delicate Balance*, and *Seascape*) suggest Albee's continuing attraction to surrealism and absurdity. As in the theatre of the absurd, which strongly influenced Albee's earliest work, and which continues to intrigue him, symbolic action is rendered literally. The characters' fears and neuroses, their failure to reach each other, their "human condition," are objectified: the abstract becomes concrete. Throughout Albee's work, suburban living rooms are transformed into arenas of combat between the real and the symbolic. Placed in an immediately recognizable, realistic setting, Albee's characters are threatened by cosmic metaphysical terrors.

Albee has been mistakenly described as a realist and a social dramatist, and although there are elements of social concern and protest in his work, Albee is primarily an absurdist for whom reality serves only as an invitation to the surreal and the fantastic. In the plays, the mundane reality that the characters cling to is mercilessly challenged and disrupted. The characters are terrifically self-protective because they are never safe. From the prim, smug Peter, comfortably settled on a park bench in *The Zoo Story*, Albee's first play, to the bland middle-aged couple enjoying a picnic on the beach in *Seascape*, characters are menaced, invaded, pursued. Like many later characters, Peter is intent on maintaining a mellow detachment from life, but his mask is pierced by an intense, insinuating outsider named Jerry.

Once characters open the doors of their usually snug, enclosed living rooms to visitors from the outside world, the delicate balance of their lives is threatened. The plays dramatize various strategies of invasion, often in the guise of routine social encounters. In *The American Dream*, for instance, a young man in a bikini and a dizzy social worker visit the apartment of an archetypal Albee family— with surprising consequences. In *Who's Afraid of Virginia Woolf?*, a young professor and his wife call on a middle-aged academic couple. In *A Delicate Balance*, best friends stop by for an unexpected visit. In *All Over*, a wealthy family awaits another kind of visitor as the family patriarch lies dying. In play after play, seemingly mundane characters and situations are invested with mysterious overtones, and the characters' masks of normality are stripped away to reveal layers of psychological deformity. The action unleashes the demons that the characters struggle to suppress. Reality collides with fantasy, literal and symbolic action clash with often startling results as Albee fuses the banal with the cosmic.

Albee's characteristic method, then, is to impose on the settings and the character types familiar from Braodway domestic realism the fanciful conceits of the theatre of the absurd. His characters are mixtures of realistic observation and a highly charged, at times grotesque theatricality. And his language is also poised, sometimes uneasily, between the real and the surreal, the ordinary and the absurd. Dialogue in Albee is both faithful to the rhythms of everyday speech and a self-conscious, manneristic heightening of it. In the course of a single speech, his characters can shift from the concrete to the abstract, from prose to poetry. Dealing with subjects that are fundamentally realistic, he then tries to create an atmosphere of mystery and obscurity. Language and theme become increasingly spare, remote. Echoing the methods of Pinter, the later Albee charges even the most seemingly ordinary conversations with an aura of menace and insinuation. In his first plays, Albee's characters probably say too much; in his most recent work, they often say too little. Like Pinter, Albee explores the possibilities of the drama of the unspoken.

Counting the Ways and *Listening,* which are the culminations of Albee's brushes with obscurity, are deliberately unclear about basic information such as where the action is taking place and what sort of connections bind the characters. In this escalating process of reduction and refinement, Albee's drama becomes a kind of secular ritual in which words are arranged in rhythmed, repeated patterns that have an incantatory quality. From the vaudevillian overwriting of the early plays to the lean, pared manner of the late chamber works, Albee's dialogue is consistently self-regarding: language in the plays always calls attention to itself.

Albee has been writing plays since 1958. His first drama, *The Zoo Story,* was given its world premiere in Berlin in 1960, and within three years, after the productions off-Broadway of his four one-acts and the Broadway presentation of *Virginia Woolf,* he was recognized as an important playwright, his name linked with those of Tennessee Williams, Arthur Miller, and William Inge. He has won two Pulitzer Prizes—for *A Delicate Balance* in 1967, and for the very lightweight *Seascape* in 1975—yet he has not in fact enjoyed a major financial and critical success since *Who's Afraid of Virginia Woolf?* (1962). The plays that established his reputation—*The Zoo Story, The American Dream,*

The Sandbox, The Death of Bessie Smith, Virginia Woolf—are written with youthful exuberance. Themes and character types that Albee will return to again and again are given spectacular introductions in his fledgling one-acts: the domineering women and impotent men who populate the canon are here dramatized with vaudevillian zest. The method is one of theatrical exaggeration. *Virginia Woolf* muted absurdist techniques to a more naturalistic level, while retaining the acerbic wit and the Strindbergian sexual combat that illuminated the first plays. Albee, though, has avoided repeating the manner of *Virginia Woolf*. He has not since written the same kind of extravagantly theatrical comedy of manners. None of his subsequent work has the coruscating sarcasm, the obvious relish for cruelty and humiliation, the rich invective of that gloriously high-strung drama of academic bad manners. Husbanding his talent for venomous domestic warfare, Albee has erased much of the naturalistic texture that underlines *Virginia Woolf* in favor of an increasingly poetic and disembodied diction. Since the pinnacle of *Virginia Woolf*, he has moved, gradually, to writing high-toned chamber dramas set among "our betters," and his work has become noticeably smaller, dryer, more airless and enclosed.

The increasingly arch and well-born voice of the plays nonetheless retains echoes of the explosive wit and deadly irony—the hilarious bitchiness—that earned Albee his high position. The collision between vernacular comedy and a high poetic mode is in fact part of the delicate balance of most of the plays. The characters, typically, slide between two levels of diction, a high-flown, self-conscious poeticizing, and a gutsy, snappy colloquialism.

Without ever losing sight altogether of a commercial base, and without simply imitating the formula of *Virginia Woolf*, each of Albee's plays since 1962 has attempted some kind of experiment. Albee has set out each time to be surprising, at times "difficult." Even his severest critics cannot accuse him of being a hack. Albee is in the curious position, however, of being accepted in the popular mind as an intellectual playwright while being attacked by many serious critics as a charlatan, a writer whose theatrical flair camouflages an impoverished intellect. Robert Brustein and Richard Schechner have been particularly virulent opponents of Albee's work, scoring the playwright for courting the Broadway crowd while masquerading as an avant-garde innovator.

Albee's plays, it is true, are not radical theatre, but they are more audacious and individual than his most hostile critics have allowed. *Tiny Alice* (1964), which remains his most ambitious work, is an elaborate allegory that mixes sex, religion, and philosophy in tantalizing, if unbalanced, doses. *A Delicate Balance* (1966), *All Over* (1971), and *Seascape* (1975) introduce thematic and stylistic variations on the archetypal Albee family. The writing in these plays is more formal and severe, and therefore decidedly less "popular," than the excoriating comic style of *Virginia Woolf*. *Box* and *Quotations from Chairman Mao Tse-Tung* (1968), *Listening* (1975), and *Counting the Ways* (1976) are chamber plays that have more in common with the methods of poetry, music, and non-representational painting than with those of traditional theatre. Albee's three adaptations from the work of other writers— *The Ballad of the Sad Cafe* (1963), from the novella by Carson McCullers; *Malcolm* (1965), from the novel by James Purdy; and *Everything in the Garden* (1967), from the play by Giles Cooper— are his least flavorful dramas, yet each play represents an experiment with theatrical style and technique. In each adaptation, Albee sets for himself a particular problem: how, in the case of *The Ballad of the Sad Cafe* and *Malcolm,* to give theatrical dimension to material conceived for another medium; and how, in the case of

Everything in the Garden, to modify the tone and sensibility of another playwright's idea. Of all these works, only *Everything in the Garden* approximates the scale and tenor of the conventional Broadway play that his harshest critics kept accusing him of writing.

Albee, then, has written the kind of play he wanted to write. His work is undertaken for personal satisfaction rather than to court popular approval, and yet at the same time the plays are curiously (and increasingly) impersonal. Unlike a dramatist like Tennessee Williams, whose plays are the expression of his own neurotic conflicts, Albee's work masks much of his own personality: we cannot "read" Albee through his writing. Williams has said that the work of a writer and the life of a writer are linked inextricably; Albee's work seems to be increasingly removed from his own most personal concerns. Albee inevitably draws on his own experiences, yet he maintains an icy, insistent distance from autobiography. His method is indirect, metaphorical. Unmarried, he writes most often about upper-middle-class marriage and the family, which he attacks with savage intensity. The typical suburban settings of his plays, as well as the recurrent image of the well-off American family as coiled and fatally incomplete, are based on Albee's own life.

Abandoned by his parents, Albee was adopted at age two by a well-to-do Westchester couple, heirs to the Keith-Albee vaudeville circuit. He grew up surrounded by governesses and nannies; as a child, he was chauffeur-driven to the theatre. Pampered, hovered over by a domineering, imperious Westchester matron, he became a rebellious child. He was expelled from a number of private schools and military academies until, at twenty, he left the comfortable suburbs to make his way in the city. For ten years, he worked at a series of ordinary jobs, living in rundown apartments and rooming houses (often with the composer William Flanagan as roommate), drifting into a literary and artistic group in Greenwich Village. In 1958, he began, at age thirty, to write plays, and his first effort, *The Zoo Story*, was about a disturbed young man who is a wanderer in the city.

Albee has always been reticent in discussing his private life. In interviews, he often adopts the pose of a cynic, making sardonic cracks at the incompetence of critics. About himself, he remains cryptic. Here, too, the comparison with Tennessee Williams is blatant. Williams's compulsive volubility about his personal affairs, his sexual peccadilloes, his neurotic fears and insecurities, his confinement in a mental institution, his gnarled family history, resulted in the wonderfully frank revelations of *Memoirs* (1975). Albee is not likely ever to be attracted to the confessional mode. His response to an epidemic of self-exposure among his contemporaries, in fact, is to burrow further into himself, to become even more private. Williams reveals his knotted personality with the flair and exhibitionism of a born showman; Albee remains the sly, sharp-tongued, brooding observer of human follies.

Albee, interestingly, has used his Westchester background more often than he has drawn on his vagabond years as an urban bohemian. The voice in play after play is that of a rebellious child raging against his rich, straitlaced parents—the arch and oppressive figure of the suburban matron haunts his imagination. Only in his first play, *The Zoo Story*, does Albee choose the social and sexual outlaw for his protagonist. The world of the dispossessed, that preoccupies Tennessee Williams, does not detain Albee beyond this initial effort; and even here, the outsider is pitted against an establishment figure rather than being presented in his own environment. In *The Zoo Story*, Albee's proper Westchester childhood and his rootless city life clash symbolically in the embattled encounter between the prim, self-protective, married Peter, and the isolated, disoriented figure of Jerry. Jerry impales himself against his own dagger, while Peter, shaken but at liberty, runs back to the shelter of his East Side apartment. Albee in this first play seems to have exorcised characters like Jerry from his work, while the rigid, put-upon Peter is a type that continues to bedevil him; the weak male controlled by powerful women resurfaces obsessively in play after play.

Albee conducts his rebellion, then, in well-appointed drawing rooms rather than in the streets. The figure of the fugitive, the vagabond, the social outsider, is virtually erased from his work in favor of the character who has the weight of family and home to bolster him and to destroy him. Jerry is a richer, more provocative character than Peter, yet Albee sets his plays in Peter's world rather than Jerry's. The kind of threat that Jerry represents to the smug Peter is transformed in later plays into the ominous forces that lurk outside the Westchester living rooms.

Jerry's threat to Peter is partly sexual, and it is typical of Albee's methods that the character's sexual history is only alluded to in passing. Sexuality in the plays is almost always indirect, sexual energy being often expressed through insult and invective. Sex in *Tiny Alice* is disguised as religious and philosophical doubt; mysticism and rhetoric are employed as barricades against the central sexual conflict that triggers the action. Albee's characters are often removed from sex; bodies in Albee are never, as they are in the work of Tennessee Williams, instruments not only of lust but of salvation and spiritual transcendence as well. The characters in the later plays especially are menopausal; they're well beyond their sexual peak, and seemingly relieved about it. Significantly, the one character in all the plays who is infatuated with his body—the bikini-clad, muscled young man who represents the American Dream in both that play and *The Sandbox*—stands outside the action as a kind of guardian angel. Albee's response to the character is ambivalent, recalling Tennessee Williams's divided attitude to *his* Adonis figures: The perfect form of the American Dream cloaks an empty spirit.

Albee has not returned (except, indirectly, in *Malcolm*), to the nightworld of the sexual underground that hovers provocatively over both *The Zoo Story* and *The American Dream*. His characters, typically, are obsessed with death rather than sex; they're more concerned with their mortality than they are with their sexuality, and impotence and finality become the standard Albee themes. There is not a single play that offers an image of sexual abundance. As Albee's work describes a preoccupation with the ends of things, with loss and defeat, it traces a sliding downward curve in evergy and impact. The nasty black comedy, the surging rhetoric, the showmanship of the earlier plays is gradually replaced by the spare and ultra-refined closet dramas—plays for orchestrated voices whose dependence on repeated phrases and images, on antiphonal responses, on calculated, twisted syntax, are more the materials of dramatic readings than the stuff of full-bodied human drama.

Albee's career to date, then, is a study in contradictions, in uneasy, delicate balances between domestic realism and absurdist theatricality, between the shocks of recognition of commercial drama and the flights of fantasy of experimental theatre, between a homespun, colloquial diction and a manneristic poeticizing, between verbal explosiveness and torrential rhetoric on the one hand and sexual and verbal abstinence and evasiveness on the other. The method has been— and continues to be—a hazardous one, rich in achievement and rife with disappointment.

II

The Living Room Wars

Albee typically uses the standard setting of Broadway comedy and drama—the comfortable suburban living room—as the deceptively conventional backdrop for his bitter attacks against the American family. From *The American Dream* to *All Over,* he creates a series of fractured, divided familes who engage in fierce domestic warfare. There is always something fatally wrong, emotionally incomplete, about the Albee family. Domestic hostilities are dramatized with ferocious and often comic literalness: parents and children act out feelings of murderous rage against each other. Parents are child-killers and child-molesters, children fantasize about having killed their parents, mothers and daughters have savage sexual rivalries, fathers and sons are virtual stangers. The plays are overrun with devouring mothers, castrating wives, remote husbands, dead sons.

In the early work, family battle is presented with the farcical exaggeration and literalness of the absurdist theatre. In *The American Dream,* the parents actually dismember their child. In *Who's Afraid of Virginia Woolf?,* the parents create and then destroy their child in a fantasy game that symbolically reflects actual parental destructiveness. In later plays, familial animosity is handled in a more muted fashion, but elemental antagonism between husbands and wives and between parents and children is still palpitantly present. Albee's view of the family remains unremitting in its harshness.

The primary Albee household is dissected, hilariously, in *The American Dream,* the playwright's most purely absurdist piece. Here, grasping Mommy, vacant Daddy, and a victimized, unloved child provide material for vaudevillian black comedy as they demonstrate their meanness and vapidity. Mommy, the chief wrongdoer, wants to get rid of Grandma, treats Daddy like an imbecile child, and has destroyed "the bumble," her only son. Grandma describes the child's dismemberment to

Mrs. Barker, a clubwoman and head of an adoption agency, who visits this far-gone household.

GRANDMA: . . . in the first place, it turned out the bumble didn't look like either one of its parents. That was enough of a blow, but things got worse. One night, it cried its heart out, if you can imagine such a thing.

MRS. BARKER: Cried its heart out! Well!

GRANDMA: But that was only the beginning. Then it turned out it only had eyes for its Daddy.

MRS. BARKER: For its Daddy! Why, any self-respecting woman would have gouged those eyes right out of its head.

GRANDMA: Well, she did. That's exactly what she did. But then, it kept its nose up in the air.

MRS. BARKER: Ufggh! How disgusting!

GRANDMA: That's what they thought. But *then*, it began to develop an interest in its you-know-what.

MRS. BARKER: In its you-know-what! Well! I hope they cut its hands off at the wrists!

GRANDMA: Well, yes, they did that eventually. But first, they cut off its you-know-what.

MRS. BARKER: A much better idea!

GRANDMA: That's what they thought. But after they cut off its you-know-what, it *still* put its hands under the covers, *looking* for its you-know-what. So, finally, they *had* to cut off its hands at the wrists. . . . And it was such a resentful bumble. Why, one day it called its Mommy a dirty name.

MRS. BARKER: Well, I hope they cut its tongue out!

GRANDMA: Of course. And then, as it got bigger, they found out all sorts of terrible things about it, like: it didn't have a head on its shoulders, it had no guts, it was spineless, its feet were made of clay . . . just dreadful things . . . for the last straw, it finally up and died; and you can imagine how *that* made them feel, their having paid for it, and all.

Mrs. Barker has come to sell Mommy and Daddy a new "bumble," who turns out to be a perfectly formed young man in a bikini—the American Dream. He represents the plastic ideal, a "bumble" of perfection guaranteed to give mommy and Daddy maximum satisfaction. The American Dream is truly their child, for, as he exlains to Grandma, "I no longer have the capacity to feel anything. I have no

emotions. I have been drained, torn asunder . . .
disemboweled. . . . I let people touch me . . . I let
them draw pleasure from my groin . . . from my
presence . . . from the fact of me . . . but, that is
all it comes to. As I told you, I am incomplete . . .
I can feel nothing. I can feel nothing. And so . . .
here I am . . . as you see me. I am . . . but this . . .
what you see. And it will always be thus." He
has found an ideal home with Mommy and
Daddy. They buy him from Mrs. Barker, and
the cycle of parental greed and lust is to be
enacted once again, as Mommy, poised for
attack, begins to fondle the delicious new
"bumble."

Albee needs the freedom of absurdist fantasy in order to express the enormity of his
rage against both the castrating, lustful
mother and the emasculated, childlike father.
The American Dream is a sour, mocking play that
flays the American itch for materialistic satisfaction, as well as the inane chit-chat and the
meaningless social niceties, of this representative family. This image of the family as a
cauldron of seething Freudian maladjustments
haunts Albee in all of his work; in different
moods and styles, he returns, obsessively, to
these destroyed and destroying figures. The
repetition that is part of the grim comedy of
this play—the family enacts the same rituals of

destruction over and over—provides one of the chief thematic links in the canon. Many of Albee's later characters, like the American Dream, are also entrapped in a mother-dominated house.

Although the child and the husband in this early play are doomed, Grandma escapes. She is sharp-tongued, ironic, hard—qualities necessary for survival in the Albee menage. Grandma uses language to defend herself; insult, skillfully delivered, is an ultimate weapon in the Albee living room. Grandma sees more clearly than the other characters. Cutting through hypocrisy, she knows the real from the artificial. And like many later mothers in Albee's work, she offers a pitiless assessment of her unlovely daughter: "It's Mommy over there makes all the trouble," she says to Daddy. "If you'd listened to me, you wouldn't have married her in the first place. She was a tramp and a trollop and a trull to boot, and she's no better now. . . . When she was no more than eight years old she used to climb up on my lap and say, in a sickening little voice, 'When I gwo up, I'm going to mahwy a wich old man; I'm going to set my wittle were end right down in a tub o' butter, that's what I'm going to do.' And I warned you, Daddy; I told you to stay away from her type."

Often speaking directly to the audience, Grandma is the sardonic mistress of ceremonies, commenting acidly on her daughter's selfishness, and on the characters' almost obscene self-ignorance. "Well, I guess that just about wraps it up," she concludes, as Mommy sidles up lasciviously to the compliant young man. "I mean, for better or worse, this is a comedy, and I don't think we'd better go any further. No, definitely not. So, let's leave things as they are right now . . . while everybody's happy . . . while everybody's got what he wants . . . or everybody's got what he thinks he wants."

In *Who's Afraid of Virginia Woolf?,* Albee reworks the neurotic conflicts of the family in *The American Dream.* Here again are a voluble, desperate, rampaging wife, a detached husband, and a helpless (and imaginary) child. As in the one-act, the parents use the child as a pawn in their own embattled relationship—the child has no identity apart from his usefulness as a projection of the parents' psychoses. The children in both plays are symptoms rather than facts—they literally don't exist.

The querulous, wrangling tone of the aboriginal Albee family in *The American Dream* is expanded in *Virginia Woolf* to full-dress bitchiness. George and Martha are more skillful battlers than Mommy and Daddy because they are more evenly matched. They exult in their capacity to be cruel to each other. The long play is sustained by their ingenious schemes to provoke and humiliate each other as well as their hapless guests, Nick and Honey. The war between George and Martha is a spectacular display of verbal sparring and oneupmanship; the play, in effect, is an extended showcase for the characters' raillery and wit.

Plots in Albee plays are mostly loose frameworks against which to set his characters snapping at each other. The story in *Virginia Woolf* is especially economical. George and Martha entertain a new faculty couple during a long night's sodden journey into day. They "perform" for Nick and Honey, who, like Mrs. Barker in *The American Dream,* are intruders whose invasion triggers family warfare. Nick and Honey are catalysts who inspire George and Martha to exhibit their monumental neuroses. George and Martha use their guests the way they use their child—as sounding boards for their complaints against each other. The young couple are naive newcomers to the college community, and their particularly vulnerable position encourages George and Martha's nastiness. Nick's easy handsomeness and obvious availablilty arouse Martha's lust; Nick's presence allows her to act the strumpet.

The guests' ingenuousness kindles George's cruelty and condescension. The guests, in short, increase their hosts' theatrical opportunities, as in this representative (blistering) exchange:

MARTHA: You know what I'm doing, George?

GEORGE: No, Martha . . . what are you doing?

MARTHA: I'm entertaining. I'm entertaining one of the guests. I'm necking with one of the guests.

GEORGE: Oh, that's nice. Which one?

MARTHA: Oh, my God you're funny. (Her balance is none too good, and she bumps into or brushed against the door chimes by the door.)

GEORGE: Someone at the door, Martha.

MARTHA: Never mind that. I said I was necking with one of the guests.

GEORGE: Good . . . good. You go right on.

MARTHA: Good?

GEORGE: Yes, good . . . good for you.

MARTHA: Oh, I see what you're up to, you lousy little . . .

GEORGE: I'm up to page a hundred and . . .

MARTHA: Cut it! Just cut it out! Goddam bongs.

GEORGE: They're chimes, Martha. Why don't you go back to your necking and stop bothering me? I want to read.

MARTHA: Why, you miserable . . . I'll show *you*.

GEORGE: No . . . show him, Martha . . . he hasn't seen it. *Maybe* he hasn't seen it. You haven't seen it yet, have you?

NICK: I . . . I have no respect for you.

GEORGE: And none for yourself, either . . . I don't know what the younger generation's coming to.

NICK: You don't . . . you don't even . . .

GEORGE: Care? You're quite right . . . I couldn't care less. So, you just take this bag of laundry here, throw her over your shoulder, and . . .

NICK: You're disgusting.

GEORGE: Because *you're* going to hump Martha, I'm disgusting?

MARTHA: You Mother!

In addition to providing an audience for George and Martha, Nick and Honey reflect their hosts' barren marriage because they too are childless. Honey keeps having hysterical pregnancies. She blows up, but her stomach is filled only with air. Honey is a mousey wife (a rare character type in Albee) terrified by the prospect of having children because she herself is an elderly child. Her father is a minister who built a fortune on fakery and illusion, and Nick, a slick opportunist whose smooth good looks and callowness echo the qualities of the American Dream, has married her only for her money, as George has married Martha because her father is President of the college. These two childless couples, for whom reality and fantasy are deeply interwoven, playact at being married.

George and Martha are wily, cagey adversaries, well practiced in verbal combat. George mocks Martha's vulgarity, her lust for younger men, her blatant need to be cared for; Martha attacks George for his failure to clumb to the top of the academic ladder, for his repressed, anti-social manner. In a typical Albee ploy, George and Martha seem to have reversed sexual roles, George castigating Martha for her brash "masculine" qualities, Martha berating George for his quiet "womanly" ways. Loud Martha, dressed in toreador pants and tight sweater, is almost a misogynist's parody of emphatic, grasping female sexuality, a portrait of a voracious female that contains both fear of her power and a muted respect for her energy as well as compassion for her needs. Albee's response to Martha is complex, and it is this sense of balance, this awareness that the character's strength and weakness are closely connected, that gives dimension to the battle and that raises George and Martha above the deliberately flat, cartoon-like and purely emblematic figures in *The American Dream*.

Braying, coarse Martha is also warm-hearted, her barbed manner a measure of her vulnerability. Unlike Mommy, who has only contempt for Daddy, Martha really loves George. Periodically, as in the following passage, Martha drops her mask:

> George; my husband. . . . George who is out somewhere there in the dark . . . George who is good to me, and whom I revile; who understands me, and whom I push off; who can make me laugh, and I choke it back in my throat; who can hold me, at night, so that it's warm, and whom I will bite so there's blood; who keeps learning the games we play as quickly as I can change the rules; who can make me happy and I do not wish to be happy, and yes I do wish to be happy. George and Martha: sad, sad, sad.

George is also created in the round. Allowing himself to be dominated, and comfortable with being an undistinguished member of the history department, George nonetheless has strength

28

in reserve. It is he, in the final bout, who claims the victory. He has always been stronger than Martha, and he has always known it.

The two of them have a rich sense of theatre, skillfully arranging the long evening as so many exercises in psychodrama. Like characters in a Pirandello play, however, they are not certain where playacting and reality merge. They orchestrate the evening in a series of separate routines: Get the Guests, Humiliate the Host, Hump the Hostess. Moving from Fun and Games in Act I, to Walpurgisnacht in Act II, to the Exorcism in Act III, their playacting becomes increasingly serious. Significantly, the final clash, precipitating a breakthrough for both George and Martha, concerns the omnipresent Albee theme of parent-child relationships. In a masterful stroke, George decides to "kill" the child they have invented. This scarred, mutilated, made-up child has served only as a way for the couple to attack each other; in killing the child, George frees himself and Martha from a crippling reliance on illusion. Martha has broken the "rules" by telling Honey, an outsider, about the kid ("the bit"), and so George gets even by exploding the fantasy.

The motif of the imaginary child has been a source of critical contention. Those who are unconvinced by it argue that the patent symbolism of the fantasy child conflicts with the play's naturalistic texture, and suggest that George and Martha ought really to be committed. As an element in a drama that is read, mistakenly, as a transcript of life, the child is of course an intrusion; but as a symbolic representation of a warped, sadomasochistic relationship, as part of the fabric of a highly theatrical and only marginally realistic domestic drama, the child is much more acceptable. On a symbolic level, the child underlines the characters' own sense of incompleteness and impotence. That Albee, however, did not entirely adjust the play's varying levels of psychological realism and literary symbolism is the key example in his work of an imperfect blend of realism and surrealism.

The parent-child motif is nonetheless central to this play, as it is to virtually all the plays. Albee expands it by including a haunting monologue in which George recalls the story of a boy who killed his parents—accidentally:

> When I was sixteen and going to prep school, during the Punic Wars, a bunch of us used to go into New York on the first day of vacations. . . . And one time, in the bunch of

us, there was this boy who was fifteen, and he had killed his mother with a shotgun some years before—accidentally, completely accidentally, without even an unconscious motivation, I have no doubt, no doubt at all—and this one evening this boy went with us, and we ordered our drinks, and when it came his turn he said, I'll have bergin . . . give me some bergin, please . . . bergin and water. Well, we all laughed . . . he was blond and he had the face of a cherub, and we all laughed, and his cheeks went red and the color rose in his neck, and the assistant crook who had taken our order told people at the next table what the boy had said, and then they laugh-ed, and then more people were told and the laughter grew, and more people and more laughter, and no one was laughing more than us, and none more than the boy who had shot his mother. . . . The following summer, on a country road, with his learn-er's permit in his pocket and his father on the front seat to his right, he swerved the car, to avoid a porcupine, and drove straight into a large tree. He was not killed, of course. And in the hospital, when he was conscious and out of danger, and when they told him that his father *was* dead, he began to laugh.

The parent-killer was placed in an asylum. "That was thirty years ago," George concludes. "And I'm told that for these thirty years he has . . . not . . . uttered . . . one . . . sound." Martha teases George about being the parent-killer, and suggests that the boy's prolonged catatonic state is symbolic of George's own introversion. Like the imaginary child, the figure of the boy who killed his mother and father symbolically reinforces aspects of the characters' unconscious longings.

Having cut their way through a thicket of verbal abuse, George and Martha reach a tentative happy ending. The husband asserts his role as master of his house, the wife acquiesces. Albee's affirmative conclusion—the play ends with a chorus of yesses, like Molly Bloom's soliloquy in *Ulysses*—has been attacked as a capitulation to Broadway sensibilities, an appeasement of middle-class convictions about the place of men and women in the home. The ending is certainly sentimental, though not entirely unprepared for since Albee has tried to indicate all along that George and Martha really do care for each other, and that their mutual baiting is a perverse expression of love. In leaving George and Martha in peace, however, exhusted and cleansed by the exorcism of the child, Albee reveals his emotional and intellectual distance from the world view of the absurdists. There are no neat resolutions in the topsy-turvy universe of Beckett or Ionesco. There are no happy endings in plays like *Waiting for Godot* and *The Bald Soprano,* which dramatize an existential condition from which there is no escape. Gogo and Didi, Beckett's tramps, continue to wait, condemned to endless repetitions of hope and frustration; their waiting is simply a grim metaphor for life's duration. Albee is unable to accept the notion of absolute meaninglessness or finality, and so, in *Virginia Woolf,* he extracts from his domestic setting, no matter how entrapped his characters may seem, some suggestions of moral redemption. Having gone to war, and having faced their illusions, George and Martha earn the chance for a repaired relationship. Albee extends to his characters the possibility of change that is not available to the protagonists in genuinely absurdist plays.

Less successful than his qualified happy ending is the playwright's attempt to place his quartet of bickering, clawing characters against an allegorical framework. George is a historian, Nick is a biologist, and both Albee (and a few critics) have made too much of this simple enough contrast, trying to twist a nasty, roaring comedy of manners into a statement about American culture. Symbol-mongers have also leapt at the implications of the name of the college town in which the action is set (New Carthage)as well as noticing that George and Martha have the first names of President Washington and his wife. In interviews, Albee himself has encouraged this kind of far-fetched and high-handed reading of the play; but *Virginia Woolf* is by no means an allegory of America's betrayal of its revolutionary principles, with inhuman scientists overtaking the humanists, the future-oriented discoveries of biologists like Nick canceling the humane antiquarian concerns of historians like George. The play's thrust is not to be found in the labored dialogue between Scientist and Historian, but in the lacerating wit of its elemental battles between husbands and wives and between parents and children.

Everything in the Garden, A Delicate Balance, and *All Over* are also set in embattled living rooms. Written in a more sober and at least seemingly realistic vein than either *The American Dream* or *Who's Afraid of Virginia Woolf?,* the plays nonetheless contain elements of fantasy and poetry. Albee matrons run these households, although they pretend they are merely their husband's or their family's trusty stewards. Jenny, in

Everything in the Garden, becomes a prostitute in order to earn the money the family needs to keep up with their high-living neighbors and friends. Agnes, in *A Delicate Balance,* turns her house into a shelter from the outside world. The Wife in *All Over,* waiting for her husband to die, keeps watch, tends the hearth, sees, as she always has, that form and custom are properly observed. In these female-dominated houses, husbands are remote and inadequate figures of distinctly secondary importance. Richard, in *Everything in the Garden,* is not able to make enough money to keep his family afloat in a fiercely competitive suburban community. Vague, comfortable, withdrawn Tobias, in *A Delicate Balance,* has simply handed over the reins to his sturdy wife. Dying behind a screen, out of sight of the audience, the Husband in *All Over* is nonetheless an ominous presence; he is, in fact, one of the few powerful male figures in Albee's work, and yet significantly he is not a character in the present action. He is an off-stage force, spectral and hovering, whose imposing career and personality are recalled by the characters. Albee is concerned with this titan only after his life's work has been completed. *All Over* reverses the usual dynamics of the Albee family in that here a powerful man has dominated the lives of Wife, Mistress,

Daughter, and Son; but regardless of where the power is, the center of interest remains for Albee with the women of the house.

As in the earlier plays set in living rooms, the three families here are invaded by an alien presence that ignites dormant tensions. In *Everything in the Garden,* an elegant Madam is the intruder; in *A Delicate Balance,* terrified best friends disrupt the family's precarious arrangement with life; in *All Over,* the specter of mortality forces the characters to summarize and to shift perspective. Reacting against invasions, the characters must confront their own incompleteness.

Although it is adapted from an English play by Giles Cooper, *Everything in the Garden* is consistent with Albee's own interests. Here again is a faltering marriage in which a couple, recalling Mommy and Daddy in *The American Dream,* are infected with the wrong values. Richard and Jenny are blatant materialists. They are as determined as the primary Albee couple in *The American Dream* to obtain "satisfaction" for their investments. Lust for money, possessions, things, overwhelms them; totally superficial, they are obsessed with something so mundane as Keeping Up With the Joneses. A distressingly average suburban couple: what was Albee's interest in them? They don't have

George and Martha's histrionic temperaments, and so their fighting is not conducted on the grand opera level of *Virginia Woolf,* but in a tone alarmingly close at times to that of situation comedy. What seems initially, however, to be a routine comedy of middle-class manners, reminiscent of the gag-ridden style of Neil Simon, escalates to a fantasy of suburban greed. The realistic social notation, as always in Albee, is injected with theatrical exaggeration: a housewife becomes a prostitute, discovers that all her friends earn extra money in the same way, and that all their husbands not only know about but even approve of their extracurricular activity. When an intruder named Jack, a rich family friend, threatens to expose the operation, the husbands, led by the enterprising Madam, Mrs. Toothe, kill Jack and then bury him in the garden, thereby giving an ironic twist to the play's title.

Although it is based on a real story of a ring of suburban housewives who were prostitutes "on the side," the play enters the realm of fantasy when the husbands and wives resort to murder to protect their business. Aware of the conflicting levels of realism and fantasy, Albee provdes the story with a theatrical framework by making Jack a genial, wry master of ceremonies who speaks directly to the audience.

After his "murder," Jack is put back together again to oversee the finale. He delivers a coy, comforting speech to the audience:

> Oh, don't get any ideas, now. I'm dead, believe me. I'm *dead*. It's amazing how dying sobers you up. Well, I certainly never thought it would be *this* way—like this; I'd imagine sliding gently from the bar stool at the club, or crashing into a truck on a curve some night, but never this. Shows you can't tell. God! Would you believe it? Mrs. Toothe, and Beryl and Cynthia and Louise? And poor Jenny? *I* wouldn't have; but, then, I'm rather selfish—self-concerned. *Was*. I must get *used* to that; past tense.

Presiding over the action, Jack reminds the audience that it is in fact seeing an allegory of greed rather than a literal, true-to-life story about characters who might be just like themselves. Albee thus changes the unremittingly harsh tone of Cooper's original by, in a sense, "taking back" the murder: Jack isn't really dead, and therefore these ordinary suburban types didn't really kill him.

Albee further softens Cooper's dark indictment of middle-class materialism by making Jack a millionaire who, ironically, has willed three and a half million dollars to his friends,

Richard and Jenny, who now will be unable to claim the money for seven years (when Jack can be declared officially dead). This last-minute ironic fillip makes light of the theme of greed that has been so insistently sounded throughout the play and also turns Richard and Jenny into a kind of cute couple that the audience is somehow supposed to like. Even though Jack's concern for his friends, shared with the audience, is laced with irony, at some level we're meant to like them too—they're good kids despite their grisly moral lapses.

Although Jenny is sweeter than the typical Albee matron, her agreeable manner masks a shrewd determination. After she starts to work, to earn some badly needed money, she becomes increasingly deceptive as well as aggressive. Women in Albee's plays can't be strong without also being arch. Female assertiveness is not presented positively; when a woman stands up for herself, she almost inevitably is a shrew, an emasculator, a deceiver.

Like other Albee couples, Richard and Jenny are victims of their role-playing and of their antiquated ideas about the place of men and women in marriage and the family. Because Richard is too proud to have his wife go to work, Jenny must be underhanded, cagey. Richard's neanderthal attitudes force Jenny to become masked and sharp. Having been trapped into playing the part of the submissive wife, she doesn't know how to be natural as anything else. Despite initial hesitations, Richard and Jenny capitulate to their acquisitive urges; they don't have the integrity to withstand the lure of Mrs. Toothe's money. They prove no worthier than their phony, status-seeking friends, and the play thus becomes a wholesale attack on middle-class consumerism. Except for the unmarried Jack, a perennial outsider, and Roger, the protagonists' sharp-tongued son, no one is spared the playwright's disapproval.

With only minor adjustments from the original, the dialogue here is the most uninflected in Albee's work. Nowhere else do his characters speak in such a close approximation of home-spun, plain folks diction:

RICHARD: May I go back out now? *Somebody's* got to get the damn lawn mowed, and I don't notice any gardeners out there waiting for me to tell them what . . .

JENNY: I've told you two thousand times: well, I've told you *two* things two thousand times; please keep cigarettes in the house . . .

RICHARD: *You're* running it.

JENNY: *When* you finish a pack, do two
  things—I've told you . . .
RICHARD:—two thousand times—
JENNY: . . . first, when you finish a pack, look
  to see if it's the last one—the last pack . . .
RICHARD: Yes, ma'am.
JENNY: And if it is, put it down to get some
  more, or tell *me* . . .
RICHARD: O.K.; O.K.
JENNY: Whenever you *do* finish a pack, don't
  forget to take the coupons off. Please? the
  coupons? We save them?
RICHARD: Did I *forget?*
JENNY: You *always* forget. We smoke these
  awful things just to get the coupons . . .

Always ready to pounce, Albee's critics claim-
ed that with *Everything in the Garden* he had
finally written the conventional Broadway
comedy that lurked beneath the layers of
symbolism and allegory of his earlier work. But
even with its crowd-pleasing touches, the
play's scathing portrait of a fatally corrupted
marriage protects it from the charge of being a
mere commodity entertainment. The piece still
has elements of the fierce social satire and the
theatrical edge that are hallmarks of Albee's
style. And Jenny's final words about the garden
have the deliberate balance and rhythm that

41

Albee uses throughout to heighten the play's realistic base:

> JENNY: I think it ought to be planted nicely, flowers and shrubs and all. Make it look like it's really lived in. It mustn't look like it's been let go. It might draw suspicion. You notice things like that.
>
> RICHARD: Yes; you do.
>
> JENNY: Gardens that have been let go. If people let them go, you know there's something wrong in the house.
>
> RICHARD: Yes.
>
> JENNY: I think it should be well planted and taken care of; kept up. I think it should look like all the others. Don't you think so?
>
> RICHARD: Yes; I think you're right.

The more elegantly spoken family in *A Delicate Balance* is also disrupted. The interference this time, in the form of a mysterious plague brought into the house by the family's best friends, is the richest and most suggestive merger in Albee's work of the real and the surreal, the concrete and the abstract. The play's details are once again deceptively "realistic." Agnes and Tobias are a comfortable suburban couple who have as a boarder Agnes's acerbic, alcoholic, and clear-sighted sister (named Claire) and who are visited periodically by their thirty-six year old daughter Julia, after one of her divorces. Awaiting another visit from Julia, who is leaving her fourth husband, they also receive a call from their best friends Harry and Edna, who drop by because they were sitting at home and became suddenly terrified. Harry and Edna, presuming on their forty-year friendship with Agnes and Tobias, ask if they can move in. Agnes and Tobias agree, reluctantly, but Harry and Edna leave after staying only two nights.

Albee embroiders the mundane details—a daughter with marital problems returns home; best friends, seized with a feeling of loneliness, drop by for some company—into a metaphysical mystery play. The realistically presented upper-middle-class living room is enlarged, symbolically, to become a refuge from the world: four people clamor to be admitted to this house. Harry and Edna's isolation assumes the allegorical dimensions of "the plague"—a death in the family, a divorce, a lost job, any small shock or reversal of fortune, as well as any cataclysmic upheaval which upsets our balance—from which no one is immune. The "delicate balance" is that arrangement we make with life to keep it at a safe distance.

The characters huddle around Agnes's hearth because she knows how to maintain the balance: she creates order. She is the most poised and the most autocratic of all the Albee matrons, and she copes so well because she has deliberately narrowed her world view. She masterfully screens out chaos by holding on to a constricted vision.

With a long, difficult, elegantly constructed periodic sentence, Agnes opens the play by talking about her fears of going around the bend, thus introducing the notion of imminent, hovering chaos that terrorizes the characters:

> What I find most astonishing—aside from that belief of mine, which never ceases to surprise me by the very fact of its surprising lack of umpleasantness, the belief that I might very easily—as they say—lose my mind one day, not that I suspect I am about to, or am even . . . nearby . . . for I'm not that sort; merely that it is not beyond . . . happening: some gentle loosening of the moorings sending the balloon adrift—and I think that is the only outweighting thing: adrift; the . . . becoming a stranger in . . . the world, quite . . . uninvolved, for I never see it as violent, only a drifting . . .

She completes her sentence after much further expansion of this imagined "drifting": what she finds most "astonishing" is her alcoholic sister

Claire, though Claire in fact is really only an afterthought to Agnes's speculations of how she might one day simply collapse. When Tobias, busy as always with the cocktails, says that there is no saner woman on earth, he knows whereof he speaks. For agnes only pretends to be vulnerable. She claims merely to decide the menu and to keep the house running while yielding to her husband the right to make all the really important decisions. But she is a steely, self-contained woman (Katharine Hepburn, arch and patrician and smug, was an ideal choice for the role in the film version of the play).

Tobias remains very much on the sidelines, an innocuous, mumbling figure, forever tending bar, until Act III, when Agnes hands him the reims. Tobias stays up all night, wrestling with a decision about what to do about Harry and Edna. It is he rather than Agnes who makes the aria-like speech that summarizes their position: what has their long friendship meant if Harry and Edna can't come to them for shelter?

You come for dinner don't you come for cocktails see us at the club on Saturdays and talk and lie and laugh with us and pat old Agnes on the hand and say you don't know

what old Toby'd do without her and we've
known you all these years and we love each
other don't we? . . . Doesn't friendship grow
to that? To love? Doesn't forty years amount
to anything?. . . . I like you, Harry, yes, I
really do, I don't like Edna, but that's not half
the point, I like you fine; I find my liking you
has limits . . . BUT THOSE ARE MY
LIMITS! NOT YOURS! The fact I like you
well enough, but not enough . . . that best
friends in the world should be something
else—more—well, that's my poverty. So,
bring your wife, and bring your terror, bring
your plague. BRING YOUR PLAGUE! I
DON'T WANT YOU HERE! YOU ASKED?!
NO! I DON'T! BUT BY CHRIST YOU'RE
GOING TO STAY HERE! . . . You've put
nearly forty years in it, baby; so have I, and if
it's nothing, I don't give a damn, you've got
the right to be here, you've earned it AND
BY GOD YOU'RE GOING TO TAKE IT!
DO YOU HEAR ME?! YOU BRING YOUR
TERROR AND YOU COME IN HERE AND
YOU LIVE WITH US! I DON'T WANT
YOU HERE! I DON'T LOVE YOU! BUT BY
GOD . . . YOU STAY!

But Harry and Edna leave, and after their
departure, Tobias asks for confirmation of his

masculinity from the trio of women who stand like sentinels, coffee cups in hand, in the arched doorway leading to the sunken living room. "Was I honest? Did I try?" he pleads. "Yes. You were honest. You tried," the strong women say, pretending to give him the image of himself he needs. After he retreats to his room, Agnes briskly re-establishes household routine. The tortuous rhythms of her closing lines echo the opening monologue, thereby enclosing the house (and the play) with Albee's gloriously mannered, endistancing rhetoric:

What I find most astonishing—aside from my belief that I will, one day . . . lose my mind—but when? Never, I begin to think, as the years go by, or that I'll not *know* if it happens, or maybe even *has*—what I find most astonishing, I think, is the wonder of daylight, of the sun. All the centuries, millenniums—all the history—I wonder if that's why we sleep at night, because the darkness still . . . frightens us? They say we sleep to let the demons out—to let the mind go raving mad, our dreams and nightmares all our logic gone awry, the dark side of our reason. And when the daylight comes again . . . . comes order with it. Poor Edna and Harry. Well, they're safely gone . . . and we'll

all forget . . . quite soon. Come now; we can
being the day.

The play's formal, rhythmed dialogue, with
its measured beat, its calculated arrangement
of pauses and repetitions and fragments, com-
plements the theme. Like Agnes, all the characters speak in a recital manner—language is
used as a means of protection and concealment;
words keep feelings in check. Agnes and Tobias
survive because of their ironic detachment.
They have ritualized their lives, so that decorum is a conscious barrier against messy
emotion. There is much small talk in the play,
chit-chat about the club, about the servant
problem, about shopping, about who wants
what to drink. Claire tells an amusing story
about her encounter with a prim saleswoman
from whom she wanted to purchase a topless
bathing suit. Some critics attacked the story as
being another example of Albee's use of slick
Broadway humor to placate his audience, but
the occurrence throughout the play of such
seemingly irrelevant anecdotes is part of the
diversionary tactics that all the characters rely
on. These people, clustered in Agnes's house
for protection against the storm, participate
eagerly in evasions; they want and need to be
distracted from contemplation of the abyss. As

protection, characters shift their tone in mid-sentence, their consideration of "the plague" that has invaded them broken by attention to a mundane domestic detail, their language plummeting from abstract philosophical speculation to colloquial badinage. Agnes's first long peroration is punctuated by domestic concerns: "What are you looking for, Tobias?" "Why on earth do you want anisette?" "I will do cognac." "Cognac is sticky." "Are you comfortable?" Agnes's semi-ironic contemplation of incipient madness is thus sprinkled with these homely parenthetical exchanges that maintain household discipline. Near the end, Agnes's lofty summing up of what has happened to them is followed by an apology about the lack of coffee:

> Time happens, I suppose. To people. Everything becomes . . . too late, finally. You know it's going on . . . up on the hill; you can see the dust, and hear the cries, and the steel . . . but you wait; and time happens. When you *do* go, sword, shield . . . finally . . . there's nothing there . . . save rust; bones; and the wind. (Pause) I'm sorry about the coffee, Edna. The help must hide the beans, or take them with them when they go to bed.

Agnes sometimes pokes fun at her own ornate manner; as when she scolds Claire for her inebriated conduct:

> *If* you come to the dinner table unsteady, *if* when you try to say good evening and weren't the autumn colors lovely today you are nothing but vowels, and *if* one smells the vodka on you from across the room—and *don't* tell me again, *either* or you! that vodka leaves nothing on the breath: if you are expecting it, if you are sadly and wearily expecting it, it *does*—*if* these conditions exist . . . . *persist* . . . then the reaction of one who is burdened by her love is not brutality— though it would be excused, believe me!— not brutality at all, but the souring side of love. If I scold, it is because I wish I needn't. If I am sharp, it is because I am neither less nor more than human, and if I am to be accused once again of making too much of things, let me remind you that it is my manner and not the matter. I apologize for being articulate.

Mrs. Toothe, the Madam in *Everything in the Garden*, says that we must forget what we have to in order to survive. *A Delicate Balance* is about that necessary forgetting, that self-willed absent-mindedness. Despite all their precautions against disorder, though, Agnes and

Tobias are invaded: the specters of divorce, alienation, and loneliness disrupt the steadfastly placid surface of their narrow, comfortable lives. But when Harry and Edna leave, Agness quickly returns her house to order. Shaken during the invasion, she puts her house together again after the aliens have been expelled: her "Come now, we can begin the day" signals the restoration. The plague has been confronted, and buried. The other characters follow Agnes's lead in this ritual of forgetting. Before their departure, Edna delivers the most mournful speech in the play: "It is sad to come to the end of it, isn't it, nearly the end; so much more of it gone by . . . than left, and still not know—still not have learned . . . the boundaries, what we may not do . . . not ask, for fear of looking in a mirror. We *shouldn't* have come. . . . For our own sake; our own . . . lack. It's sad to know you've gone through it all, or most of it, without . . . that the one body you've wrapped your arms around . . . the only skin you've ever known . . . is your own—and that it's dry . . . and not warm." And right after this dark revelation, Edna asks Anges if she wants to go into town shopping on Thursday. The invitation, casually made, casually refused (but with the promise of a future trip into town) is a willful covering up, a way of ignoring the failure of a forty-year friendship.

A Delicate Balance is a play about limits. In marriage. Between parents and children. Between best friends. The order in Agnes's house is based on the observance of clearly defined boundaries. When limits are challenged, the characters inevitable fail each other. Children ask more from parents than parents are able to give; best friends of a lifetime can offer only so much help, and no more. No one in this house cares deeply, or ultimately, about anyone else; and "the plague" forces them all to recognize their distance from each other. The play is Albee's most compassionate treatment of the family as a divided, incomplete, and isolating social group.

The besieged family is a typical Albee menage. Strong, dominant matron; ineffectual, private father; a dead son; a bitter sibling rivalry; a strained parent-child relationship. In this loveless household, each person is possessive about his own room. Bedrooms become symbols of refuge and security, as well as of isolation. Claire, who often stands outside the action, commenting tartly on the characters' weaknesses, talks to Tobias about "the full house" in which people are both together and apart: "Are you going to stay up, Tobias? Sort of a nightwatch, guarding? *I've done it.* The breathing, as you stand in the quiet halls, slow and heavy? And the special . . . warmth, and . . . permeation . . . of a house . . . asleep? When the house is sleeping? when the people *are* asleep? . . . . And the difference? The different breathing and the cold, when every bed is awake . . . all night . . . very still, eyes open, staring into the dark? Do you know that one?"

Julia becomes hysterical when Harry and Edna are given *her* room. Everyone except Claire is displaced because of the guests. Tobias returns to Agnes's room, after years of sleeping in separate rooms. Harry and Edna also share a room after many years of sleeping alone. These two middle-aged couples, for whom sexual desire is only a dim memory, are forced to face their distance from each other. The shifting of bedrooms, like the plague which Harry and Edna bring with them, only reinforces the characters' sense of their estrangement. In *A Delicate Balance,* any confrontation or change is a bitter reminder of limits, of chasms between people that cannot be crossed.

The characters' fight to maintain their own rooms is emblematic of their extreme isolation. This literal separation between characters is a recurrent motif in Albee's work: the cages that separate animals and humans in *The Zoo Story;* the boxes in *The American Dream* and in *Box/ Mao/Box.* Many of Albee's people inhabit their own individual boxes, imperfectly communicating through bars and cages.

The warfare in this house, though far quieter than that in George and Martha's, reveals deeper divisions. *A Delicate Balance* is a darker play than *Who's Afraid of Virginia Woolf?* Albee ends the earlier play on an affirmative note. George and Martha really do care for each other, after all. We are given no such assurances about Agnes and Tobias, who merely have an agreement not to challenge each other: they've settled in. The other relationships are even less happy. Agnes and Julia despise each other (Albee always sees the mother-daughter relationship as especially treacherous); Agnes and Claire can barely tolerate each other's presence; Agnes and Tobias do not really care very much for Harry and Edna. George and Martha's mutual baiting was a kind of love duet, whereas here the sarcastic exchanges contain no underlying currents of love or affection. The people in this house need each other for protection against "the plague," against being adrift, but they don't really like each other.

The people in *A Delicate Balance* are too controlled to engage in the flamboyant games with which George and Martha lacerate each other; the social politeness of this later household is, on one level, what the play is all about. Agnes and Tobias are much colder than George and Martha, and they are therefore less popular and accessible as dramatic characters. Formal, chilly Agnes is an archetypal WASP. Albee removes any ethnic traces from these haughty, well-born characters, and *A Delicate Balance,* like most of his plays, confirms popular notions about WASPS as rigid, bland, emotionally stingy people who speak without accents and have no noticeable facial irregularities—they're masks of politeness broken by sporadic eruptions of venom and bitchiness.

Richly allusive in language and theme, its concrete, realistic details pivoted against suggestive metaphysical mysteries, *A Delicate Balance* is Albee's finest play, a severe and poignant statement about ultimate human isolation. The play contains the abstraction in both language and theme that had been evident from the novice one-acts and that is increasingly emphasized in the later work. *All Over* and *Seascape* are further displays of cosmic reverberations issuing from deceptively realistic domestic settings.

The two dramas are companion pieces that developed from one-acts called *Life* and *Death*. The plays indicate Albee's growing infatuation with verbal and thematic spareness, and the two works contain only remote echoes of his early flamboyance, his gaudy, outrageous theatricality. *All Over* is a sober variation on the family setting of *A Delicate Balance*. This time the threat to the family's equilibrium is the imminent death of its patriarch; the Doctor's words which end the play, "All over," are implicit from the beginning. With faint reminiscences of Beckett and Ionesco, the play dramatizes a condition of waiting, as the characters prepare themselves for the change—the freedom and release—promised by the powerful old man's demise.

Like the family group in *A Delicate Balance*, each character is locked firmly into a role. Each one occupies an almost ceremonial position, named according to his or her connection to the dying man. The Wife, the Son, the Daughter, the Best Friend (along with the Doctor and the Nurse) enact the roles as well as the feelings assigned to them by virtue of their station. Each character knows exactly what his place is, and so there is no testing, as in *A Delicate Balance*, of the limits that the characters must observe. As the Best Friend explains, they participate in a ritual of waiting, their behavior governed by "custom": "Family. Isn't it one of our customs? That if a man has not outlived his wife and children—will not outlive them . . . they gather?. . . . And we do it—custom—wanted, or not."

All Over is a play of recollection rather than confrontation, and as a result it has much less tension than either *Virginia Woolf* or *A Delicate Balance.* The play is a showcase of set speeches in which characters recall dramatic moments, minor epiphanies that summarize their attitudes and their "style." As they wait for the inevitable death, they each review significant events from the past. The Mistress recalls a long-ago summer affair with an extraordinarily handsome young man. The Wife remembers "the young girl that I was when he first came to me," and her visit t the hospital when her husband's eyes retreated from her, "going out" although they remained open. The Best Friend recounts details of his wife's nervous breakdown, and his bizarre recent chance encounter with her in a passing car. The Son tearfully reports his visit to his father's bathroom, which reminded him of his childhood. The Daughter speaks in a crisp, defensive manner about her degrading marriage.

Almost all the characters punctuate the rambling conversation with reminiscences of past deaths they have either witnessed or heard about. The Mistress recalls her grandfather, who lived to one hundred and three, and who "was not at all like those centenarians you're always reading about: full head of snow-white hair, out chopping wood all the time when they weren't burying their fourth wife or doing something worthy in the Amazon; not a bit of it. He was a wispy little man, whom none of us liked very much . . . he fell, when he was seventy-two, and did to his pelvis what you would do to a teapot were you to drop it on a flagstone floor . . . he took to his bed—or was taken there—and remained in it for thirty-one years." The Wife remembers the death of her aunt, "a moody lady, but with cause. She died when she was twenty-six—died in the heart, that is, or whatever portion of the brain controls the spirit; she went on, all the appearances, was snuffed out, finally, at sixty-two, in a car crash, all done up in jodhpurs and a derby. . . ."

The reveries provide sombre and at times lyrical passages—the writing has a lovely, chiseled quality, a beguiling sense of cadence and melody. But the reminiscences supply mood and texture without enlarging our understanding of the characters; the details often seem arbitrary, or of a purely private significance to Albee himself. One of The Wife's speeches, elegant and spare, indicates the play's often remote quality:

> I was dreaming of so many things, odd and . . . well, that I was shopping, for a kind of thread, a brand that isn't manufactured any more, and I knew it, but I thought that they might have some in the back. I couldn't remember the name of the maker, and of course that didn't help. They showed me several that were very much like it, one in particular that I almost settled on, but didn't. They tried to be helpful; it was what they used to call a dry goods store, and it was called that, and I remember a specific . . . not smell, but scent the place had, one that I only remember from being little, so I was clearly in the past. . . .

For all its formal beauty (or perhaps because of it), the speech does nothing to clarify or extend the characterization of the Wife. Its placement at this point in the play is without context—it is simply a kind of resting place. Like many of the set speeches, this is an evocative recital, ripe with nuances that remain unexplored.

Characterization is thus a mosaic of memories and impressions. Relationships have congealed long before the curtain rises, and so dramatically the play has nothing to work out or to resolve. It is a holding action, in which the characters are suspended until the Doctor delivers his long-awaited annoucement of finality. The retrospective quality of the monologues is an avoidance of dramatic conflict. Albee deliberately frees himself of the tight narrative framework, the pattern of arrival and departure, that he used in *A Delicate Balance.* As in the theatre of the absurd, he has simplified his methods by portraying a situation, a condition—waiting for the death of the patriarch. But the act of waiting here, unlike that in *Waiting for Godot,* isn't charged with existential impact. Waiting for the end in *All Over* doesn't have the cosmic dimensions of waiting that are suggested by the immobility of Beckett's clowns.

The play reveals nothing original or startling about death; as a concept, a theme, "dying" yields few insights. The characters aren't transformed or enlarged as a result of their ordeal, and so neither, of course, is the audience. At one point, the Doctor introduces a provocative idea—that the dying "become enraptured" by the source of their "closing down." To demonstrate that the dying fall in love with their executioners, he recalls his own early experiences as a doctor in prisons:

> I was with them (the men condemned to die); stayed with them; helped them have what they wanted for the last time. I would be with them, and they were alone in the death cells, no access to each other, and the buggery and the rest; and there were some, in the final weeks, who had abandoned sex, masturbation, to God, or fear, or some enveloping withdrawal, but not all; some . . . some made love to themselves in a frenzy—indeed, I treated more than one who was bleeding from it, from such—and several confided to me that their masturbation image was their executioner . . . some fantasy of how he looked.

The Doctor himself, now eighty-six, wants to reach out to his grandson and great-nephew, who recently told him, "Eighty-six! Man, that means going out!" They have reprimanded him with his mortality, and he wants to lie in their "long blond hair, put my lips there in the back of the neck, with the blond hair over me . . . You see: I suddenly loved my executioners . . . well, figuratively; and in the way of . . . nestling up against them, huddling close—for we do seek warmth, affection even, from those who tell us we are going to die, or when." These beautifully orchestrated passages, so closely controlled in tone and diction, remain self-sufficient units; the Doctor's is an isolated, interesting perception that has no tangible connection to the death that the play is ostensibly concerned with.

The play's setting, a dark, rich, forbidding drawing room, and its patrician, articulate characters, do not support the author's universalizing intentions. These characters are not important enough to merit the symbolic weight of Wife, Son, Daughter, Mistress, Best Friend, that Albee has burdened them with. Lacking the poignance and warmth, the palpitating, vulnerable humanity of Beckett's clowns, Albee's embittered, crusty Protestants are not congenial as Everyman figures. Placed on the big stage, in a setting and situation that strain for allegorical significance, this version of the fractured Albee family looks particularly theadbare.

The cast of characters is really too familiar from Albee's earlier work to withstand the symbolic heightening that it is subjected to. The Wife, virtually interchangeable with Agnes (both characters were created by Jessica Tandy in the original Broadway productions), is a haughty matron for whom both love and sexuality are faint memories. She has played her part as the Wife, keeping up appearances while her husband's affections were elsewhere. She is on good terms with the Mistress because, being so remote from her husband, she has no reason to feel jealous. Playacting the Wife has been enough for her. Like Agnes she clings to surfaces, to decorum, to order and routine, as protections against chaos—as so much insurance against the void. She is not a likable character (who among Albee's charactters is?); and Albee observes her with detachment. Brittle, deeply private, a composed matron who will not allow herself to be unsettled, she is, like the other characters, a mask in a kind of tribal pageant of well-to-do American WASPS.

The Mistress, sensual, tough, practical, vaguely reminiscent of Martha, is potentially one of Albee's most vital characters. Her natural exuberance is muted, however, because of the play's funeral parlor atmosphere. It's as if Albee chose this setting in order to establish distance between himself and his characters, and between his characters and the audience. So, in context, the Mistress must be downplayed, her caustic wit, her lustiness, held carefully in check. Confronted with death, the characters become mournfully introspective. Distinct limits to feelings and response are set. Albee seems almost to have chosen "death" as his theme as a safeguard against writing an energetic drama.

Betrayals, jealousies, struggles, have been enacted off-stage, in the past. The Best Friend has lost his wife, has had his affair with the Wife. The Wife and the Mistress have long since made their peace. The only present conflict, the only relationship not conducted in a valedictory tone, is the one between the Wife and the Daughter. Their extreme bitterness toward each other threatens to upset the play's elegiac aura. Typical of Albee's mothers, the Wife despises her children, her shrill, nagging, immature, miserably married Daughter (even more morbid and whining than Julia, in *A Delicate Balance*) and her weak, useless Son (the spiritual heir to all the mealy-mouthed, female-dominated daddies in Albee's plays). The antagonism between the Wife and her children, especially the animosity between mother and daughter, is elemental. In the encounters between the two women, the play takes on an edge of rage that differs sharply from the lyrically poised quality of most of the writing. The most memorable action in the play (perhaps because it breaks the static mood) is when

mother and daughter exchange slaps. Here, in
a single theatrical gesture, is the quintessence
of Albee's cynical attitude toward "family feeling."

Without a compelling theme or a dynamic
dramatic conflict, the play depends on "fine
writing" to sustain it. The characters all speak
in that lordly mandarin style that prevails in
the later Albee living rooms. The characters
are conscious of speaking well, and the distinc-
tion, made in the beginning, between the
words "death" and "dying," indicates the play's
often pedantic, precious tone (which is sometimes charming, sometimes not). The Mistress
recalls:

> He put down his fork, one lunch, at *my* house
> . . . what had we been talking about?
> Maeterlinck and that plagiarism business, I
> seem to recall, and we had done with that
> and we were examining our salads, when all
> at once he said to me, 'I wish people wouldn't
> say that other people "are dead." ' I asked
> him why, as much as anything to know what
> had turned him to it, and he pointed out that
> the verb to be was not, to his mind, appro-
> priate to a state of . . . non-being. That one
> cannot . . . *be* dead. He said his objection was a
> quirk—that the grammarians would scoff—

but that one could be dying, or have died . . .
but could not . . . be . . . dead.

Even more than in *A Delicate Balance,* the
converstation, idling, sometimes trifling, sea-
soned with inessential details, functions as a
kind of stopgap, a way of not confronting pain,
a means of hiding feeling. These characters are
as afraid of change and of "the plague" as those
in the earlier play. As the Daughter comments:
"Everyone's the target of something, something unexpected and maybe even stupid. You
can shore yourself up beautifully, guns on
every degree of the compass, a perfect sur-
round, but when the sky falls in or the earth
gives way beneath your feet . . . so what? It's all
untended, and what's it guarding?"

Themes are announced, explored, abandoned, returned to, much in the manner of a
musical composition. Phrases and images are
repeated—these leitmotifs underline the ritualistic nature of the drama. The diction is
simple; Albee's characters use plain words, for
the most part, but they speak in convoluted
sentences, their syntax broken and fragmented, elliptical. As in the novels of Ivy Compton-
Burnett and the plays of Pinter, Albee creates a
charged atmosphere in which a spare vocab-
lary is made to carry unexpected meanings and

associations. The language implies more than it states directly. Like Chekhov, Albee works for a reverberant subtext, a drama beneath the surface, but unlike Chekhov's, his characters here don't have the complexity, the rich inner lives, that can sustain such an indirect method. Arranging plain words in rhythmic, repeated patterns, Albee has constructed a tenebrous drama of nuance and implication. In *All Over,* the Albee living room is used more abstractly than ever before, as the setting for a timeless theme. A sense of the terminal hovers over the play itself, however, as well as the characters: Albee has by now really exhausted this particular setting and this particular configuration of characters.

It is not surprising, therefore, that his subsequent play, *Seascape,* leaves the confines of the drawing room for an exterior landscape, and drops the wrangling, chilly, emblematic characters for people with names (Nancy and Charlie) who overturn the themes of depletion and finality, and the obsessive concern with mortality, that bedeviled Albee in *Box/Mao/Box* and *All Over.* In pointed contrast to "all over," the final (lovely) word in *Seascape* is "begin." Unlike the "beginning" with which *A Delicate Balance* concludes—Agnes's "Come now, we can begin the day," has a mournful ring to it, carrying suggestions of dulled routine—the commencement in *Seascape* is a genuine affirmation. This is Albee's brightest, sweetest play—his only good natured piece to date, in fact. Nancy is a refreshingly different kind of Albee matron. She is still in love with her husband, and she expresses that love directly, without any mediating sarcasm—there are no shades of *Virginia Woolf* in this sunny seaside setting. Middle-aged, her children grown, most of her life's work completed, her purpose served, Nancy wants adventure. Unique in the canon, she is an optimist. "I love the water, and I love the air," she serenades her husband, "and the sand and the dunes and the beach grass, and the sunshine on all of it and the white clouds way off, and the sunsets and the noise the shells make in the waves and, oh, I love every bit of it. Charlie." Quite unlike Anges in *A Delicate Balance* and the Wife in *All Over,* she has no investment in arranging her life in neat patterns. Bored with symmetry, she positively beckons disorder. She wants to travel from beach to beach, to become a seaside nomad enjoying long, lazy days in the sun. She challenges Charlie to go to the depths of the ocean, as he used to do when he was a kid. "Be young again; my God, Charlie, be young!" Charlie himself has lost, or misplaced, that magical sense of discovery he had when he was a child:

> I used to lie on the warm boulders, strip off
> . . . learn about my body; no one saw me;
> twelve, or thirteen. And I would go into the
> water, take two stones, as large as I could
> manage, swim out a bit, tread, look up one
> final time at the sky . . . relax . . . begin to go
> down. Oh, twenty feet, fifteen, soft landing
> without a sound, the white sand clouding up
> where your feet touch, and all around you
> ferns . . . and lichen. You can stay down
> there so long! You can build it up, and last . . .
> so long, enough for the sand to settle and
> the fish come back. And they do—come back,
> all sizes, some slowly, eyeing past; some
> streak, and you think for a moment they're
> larger then they are, sharks, maybe, but they
> never are, and one stops being an intruder,
> finally—just one more object come to the
> bottom, or living thing, part of the undula-
> tion and the silence. It was very good.

Encouraging adventure, seeking the unfamil-
iar, Nancy is the one Albee character, apart
from the crazed and anti-social Jerry of *The Zoo
Story,* who welcomes the challenge of that other
realm, that framework of mystery and the

unknown, that terrifies most of Albee's people. Consistent with the play's surprisingly rose-colored texture, the mysterious element here, unlike the American Dream, the imaginary child, or the plague, is light-hearted, fantastic in a purely comic way: two lizard-like creatures, who speak cultivated English, emerge from the sea to startle and ultimately to delight the suburban picnickers. Far from exotic, Leslie and Sarah reflect aspects of conventional Nancy and Charlie, and in their buoyant curiosity, their naivete and charm, suggest new possibilities for the middle-aged couple now facing a great empty future. Leslie and Sarah may be sea creatures with big fishlike tails, but they squabble and carry on like typical suburban young marrieds. In his concept of giant lizards as just plain floks, Albee links the twin threads of the fantastic and the familiar that figure in all his work.

Seascape indicates, like *All Over*, Albee's continuing simplification of materials. Act I is a dialogue between Nancy and Charlie on random subjects— retirement, future prospects, recollected fragments of a mostly happy life together. Act II presents the encounter between the humans and the outsiders. The structure has an almost skeletal bareness and simplicity. The tone is much less formal than in *All Over*—banter rather than recitation is the dominant mode, although the syntax is often as tortuous as in the earlier, more rigid play, and once again characters apologize for being colloquial: "You are *not* going to live forever, to coin a phrase," Nancy reminds Charlie. "Nor am I, I suppose, come to think of it, though it would be nice; nor do I imagine we'll have the satisfaction of doing it together." In this representative little speech, simple thoughts are elevated through Albee's ornate and meandering rhythms.

The relationship established between Nancy and Charlie in Act I is joking, easy, yielding, yet with intimations of that nagging sense of isolation that overtakes so many of Albee's characters. Their rambling talk is disrupted, abruptly, by the appearance of the supernatural creatures. The play's symbolically charged, open-air setting and the couple's free-floating, teasing converstion, with its fair share of convoluted syntax, its elliptical connections between thoughts, have created an atmosphere that is loose enough, and distanced enough from reality, to accommodate the shift of tone instigated by the lizards' entrance. The materialization of the sea creatures is still meant to be a jolt, a playful version of the kind of surprise and dissonance that Albee has always delighted in. These talking lizards are a comic counterpart to the imaginary child in *Virginia Woolf*— an absurdist element thrown audaciously into a deceptively ordinary context. Like the child, the lizards represent symbolic extensions of the characters' suppressed feelings. Many critics found the fish as unacceptable as the made-up child, and charged Albee with mixing genre and tone. But Albee deflates the absurdist premise of talking fish by treating them lightly, as charming and rather small-minded. The confrontation between the human couple and the sea creatures is certainly ripe with cosmic overtones, but instead of writing a big, windy play about man's evolution, Albee has fashioned a deliberately lightweight piece, a "cosmic" comedy of quite slender proportions. An epic theme is reduced to the scale of domestic comedy, and so *Seascape* is yet another example of Albee holding himself in, of setting distinct limits on his skill and daring, while at the same time playing impish pranks on his audience. The device of talking sea creatures is in itself a bold choice for a major playwright presenting his wares in a big Broadway house (the Shubert, normally reserved for musicals) with famous actors (Deborah Kerr, Barry Nelson, Frank Langella) in the leading roles. Yet instead of a spectacular philosophical drama with the attempted scope, say, of his own *Tiny Alice,* Albee tried to court Broadway audiences with a cozy domestic fable, easily accessible in both language and sensibility. The premise of *Seascape,* then, is brave, experimental; its treatment appealing, but disappointingly tame.

The commonplaceness of much of the Act II encounter between humans and aliens is deliberate. Albee is trying to undercut the fantasy premise with gags and the little shocks of recognition of conventional situation comedy. He clearly relishes the dissonance created in handling a potentially weighty subject in a fanciful and capricious style. The small talk, the domesticity of the two couples, the petty arguing—all familiar Albee motifs—are here used to offset the dotty science fiction framework, to anchor the fantastic in the mundane.

Like the characters in *A Delicate Balance* and *All Over,* the humans and the lizards are especially self-conscious about how they speak. The situation itself compels them to check their every word, and the resulting minute scrutiny about usage is a pet subject of the playwright's. Much of Act II is concerned with linguistic analysis. *Seascape* becomes a play of and about words as Nancy and Charlie explain to Leslie and Sarah the meaning of key words and gestures. A comedy of evolution is transformed into a comic lesson in verbal and gestural communication.

NANCY: Oh; we ... well, we shake hands ... flippers, uh, Charlie?

CHARLIE: When we meet we ... take each other's hand, or whatever, and we ... touch.

SARAH: Oh, that's *nice.*

LESLIE: What for?

SARAH: Oh, Leslie!

LESLIE: I want to know what *for.*

CHARLIE: Well, it *used* to be, since most people are right-handed, it used to be to prove nobody had a weapon, to prove they were friendly.

LESLIE: We're ambidextrous.

CHARLIE: Well, that's *nice* for you. Very nice.

NANCY: And some people used to hold on to their sex parts, didn't you tell me that, Charlie?, that in olden times people used to hold on to their sex parts when they said hello ... their own?

CHARLIE: I don't think I told you quite that. Each other's maybe.

NANCY: Well, no matter. Let's greet each other properly, all right? I give you my hand, and you give me your . . . what *is* that? What is that called?

LESLIE: What?

NANCY: That there.

LESLIE: It's called a leg, of course.

NANCY: Oh. Well, we call this an arm.

LESLIE: You have four arms, I see.

CHARLIE: No; she has two arms. And two legs.

SARAH: And which are the legs?

NANCY: These here. And these are the arms.

LESLIE: Why do you differentiate?

NANCY: Why do we differentiate, Charlie?

CHARLIE: Because they're the ones with the hands on the ends of them.

NANCY: Yes.

SARAH: Go on, Leslie; do what Nancy wants you to. What is it called?

NANCY: Shaking hands.

This representative passage indicates the chatty, frothy tone of the encounter: these are average, well-meaning, exasperating suburbanites.

Like *All Over*, *Seascape* was developed from a one-act play. The derivation of *All Over* was called *Death;* the source for *Seascape* was called, appropriately enough, *Life.* The later play is as airy as the earlier play is heavy, and both works, despite much elegant writing, seem incomplete. In both, dramatic conflict is minimized in favor of word games, experiments with circuitous syntax and poetic imagery. Albee really has little to say on the grand themes of life and death, so that the plays seem like clever variations designed to cover up a hollow core—cunning theatrical inventions that make predictable points about their large, abstract subjects. The plays are extended variations on their final words, Leslie's "Begin," and the Doctor's "All Over," and although Albee's strategies are intermittently effective, almost always beautifully orchestrated for tone and rhythm, the overall impression is one of thinness. These outlinings of abstract themes lack the immediacy of Albee's Strindbergian plays about elemental antagonism between men and women. In his earlier dramas, Albee seemed to be working off grudges against kinds of people he couldn't stand, and the anger and stridency of the writing had a powerful, personal energy behind it. *All Over* and *Seascape* are, in comparison, detached, refined, written not out of intense private grievances, but from more removed and almost academic interests in Beginnings and Endings. Because the themes of life and death do not come from the playwright's own private rage, his own antipathies, the plays miss the throbbing verbal and theatrical impact of Albee's most engaged work.

III

Evasions of Drama:
The Chamber Plays

From *The American Dream* and *Tiny Alice* to the recent *Counting the Ways* and *Listening,* Albee has been infatuated with generalization and abstraction. Even in the relatively naturalistic (and specific) *Who's Afraid of virginia Woolf?,* Albee embellishes the four-character clash with broad statements about science and history, and about the Decline of the West, attempting unsuccessfully to yoke his private drama to large social and public issues. In his later work, Albee's interest in generalizing is reflected not so much by the spurious kind of social gloss that disfigures his absurdist comedies but by sidestepping the machinery of naturalistic theatre. *Box/Mao/Box, Counting the Ways,* and *Listening* are really plays for disembodied voices *(Listening* was written for radio) that arrogantly disregard storylines and traditional development of characters. The characters—the voices—in these dramas have no names, being merely designated as He or She, the Woman or the Man, and they live in a kind of timeless present in which they recollect fragments of traumatic past experiences. We are told as little as possible about the characters, who each occupy their separate boxes; and direct contact between characters is either minimal or non-existent. The drama is based more on what is left out, or on what is merely implied, than on direct conflict or confrontation.

Abandoned in spare, unlocalized settings, removed from conventional dramatic tensions and clashes, these nameless characters engage in ritualistic word games and clever verbal counterpoint. Albee's elimination of theatrical elements—his stubborn conviction that less is more—forces us to attend to his experiments with language, in which a lean, seemingly bare diction rumbles with ambiguity and nuance. Albee's rigorously trim language, his simple words often arranged in fractured, circuitous sentences, compels us to listen closely, more closely in fact than we are usually called upon to do in the theatre. The characters' cryptic utterances are often surprisingly dense; the convoluted syntax mirrors convoluted thought processes, and we must be alert in order to follow the curve of the playwright's thematic and verbal progressions. Relying more on the methods of the poet than those of the playwright, Albee builds these chamber dramas out of a few scattered images and phrases; rhythm, repetition, pattern, counterpoint, replace traditional dramatic narrative. In these deeply private, introverted, ethereal chamber plays, Albee assumes the role of an exacting taskmaster, demanding hard, close work from his actors and his audience.

Box/Mao/Box, typical of this late mannerist phase of Albee's work, is a mosaic of impressionistic images. The stage is occupied by the framework of an empty box, the outline of a large cube. As counterpoint to this frozen, uninhabited image, Albee adds a poetic recitation spoken by a women's off stage voice, which is by turns ironic, whimsical, sentimental, and mournful. Her soliloquy, which tells no story and has no characters, is a threnody of loss and annihilation, a hymn of apocalyptic doom made up of a series of disparate images, of chanted words and phrases that tease the audience with a semblance of gnomic insights:

- Box.
- Many arts: All craft now . . . and going further.
- System as conclusion, in the sense of method as an end.
- Seven hundred million babies dead in the time it takes, took, to knead the dough to make a proper loaf.
- Progress is merely a direction, movement.
- Beautiful, beautiful box.
- Or was it the milk?
- It's the little things, the *small* cracks.
- Yes, when art hurts. . . .
- The release of tension is the return to consonance; no matter how far traveled, one comes back, not circular, not to the starting point, but a . . . setting down again, and the beauty of art is order—not what is familiar, necessarily, but order . . . on its own terms.
- A billion birds at once, black net skimming the ocean. And one below them, moving fast in the opposite way!
- What was it used to frighten me? Bell buoys and sea gulls; the *sound* of them, at night, in a fog, when I was very young.

- Well, we can exist with *anything; with*out.
- Room enough for a sedia d'ondalo.
- Then the corruption is complete.

These images, aphorisms, reminiscences, their meanings imprecise, elusive, scattered in fragments throughout the woman's recital, are fused into a melodic structure that conveys a sense of finality, of ultimate doom and isolation. The single, lonely voice, sadly recollecting wholesale death and corruption, and musing on the decline of art, is underscored by the isolated cube that is the only picture the audience is given: voice and image combine in melancholy counterpoint.

"Box" itself has several connotations. It is an image of separation and confinement. It suggests a funeral casket. It recalls the shape of the theatre, the theatrical box, in which the play is being performed. It implies the intricacy of Chinese puzzles, which contain boxes within boxes—the maze within the maze is a structure Albee used in *Tiny Alice.* Boxes figure prominently in *The American Dream.* Grandma's boxes, which contain her possessions accumulated in the course of a lifetime, are also emblematic of her imminent death—the handsome young man, an emissary of death, has come to remove them. As a controlling metaphor, "box" is rich with inimations of restriction and mortality.

For the interrelated play of *Quotations from Chairman Mao Tse-Tung*, the onstage box is transformed into the deck of a luxury liner, on which there are four characters: Long-Winded Lady, Minister, Chairman Mao, and an Old Woman. Only the Long-Winded Lady and the silent Minister belong, naturalistically, to the set; the other two characters, who take no cognizance of the Long-Winded Lady or of each other, are included to provide tonal counterpoints to the woman's monologue. On one level, the play is a literal demonstration, in the manner of absurdist theatre, of the separateness of boxes, since each of the four characters occupies his own distinctly private space. The play presents concrete evidence of the failure of human communication as well as of the masks that language provides: talking past each other, these three voices hide behind the way they use words.

Mao speaks in political cliches, intoning about the necessity of overthrowing the twin mountains of imperialism and feudalism that enchain the Chinese people. His platitudinous oration is filled with contradictions since, while ostensibly preaching peace, he proclaims the need for just wars: "History shows that wars are divided into two kinds, just and unjust. We Communists oppose all unjust wars that impede progress, but we do not oppose progressive, just wars. Not only do we Communists not oppose just wars, we actively participate in them. All wars that are progressive are just, all wars that impede progress are unjust." In calling for "the devastation of the Enemy," Mao evokes an image of mass annihilation, one of the leitmotifs in *Box*. His socialist gospel recalls as well the repeated statement in *Box*, which the woman attributes to the Pope, that "so long as there are some with nothing, we have no right to anything."

Albee quotes directly from Mao's speeches, adding no new material of his own. He is not a political writer, and he includes Mao for purely formalist reasons, to provide an ironic verbal counterpoint to the character he is really interested in, and the only one for whom he wrote original dialogue—the Long-Winded Lady. Mao's flat, plodding, cliche-ridden political oratory supplies a background hum, a continuing basso profundo, against which to place the voice of the main speaker.

The Old Woman is also presented for ironic contrast. She recites a poem, "Over the Hill to the Poorhouse," by Will Carleton, the doggerel rhymes and homely sentiments of which offer

a staccato underpinning to Mao's lofty pronouncements.

> CHAIRMAN MAO: Poverty gives rise to
> the desire for change, the desire for action
> and the desire for revolution. . . .
> OLD WOMAN: Over the hill to the poor-
> house—I can't quite make it clear!
> Over the hill to the poor-house—it seems
> so horrid queer!
> Many a step I've taken, a-toilin' to and fro,
> But this is a sort of Journey I never
> thought to go.

Mao's windy rheotic and the Old Woman's
childlike rhymes offset the diction of the Long-
Winded Lady, who is another version of the
Albee Westchester matron. Albee plays off one
voice against another, often for comic juxtaposition:

> CHAIRMAN MAO: The communist ideo-
> locical and social system alone is full of
> youth and vitality, sweeping the world
> with the momentum of an avalanche and
> the force of a thunderbolt.
> LONG-WINDED LADY: Exactly: plut!

The Long-Winded Lady's monologue is the
play's thematic and linguistic centerpiece; her

twin themes of falling and dying resolve the dissonant chords sounded by Mao's cataclysmic revolutionary pronouncements, by the Old Woman's sad-comic recitation of impoverished old age, and by the sense of irretrievable loss that filters through *Box*. The Long-Winded Lady compulsively recalls two traumatic incidents, the time she fell off the deck of an ocean liner (similar to the one she is now standing on), and the agonizing process of her husband's death from cancer. The details of her fall are recounted elliptically. She begins her story in fragments that make little sense: "Well, I daresay it's hard to comprehend . . . I mean: *I* . . . at this remove . . . *I* find it hard to, well, not comprehend, but believe, or accept, if you will. So long ago! So much since. But there is was: Splash! . . . . Well, not splash, exactly, more sound than that, more of a . . . no, I can't do that—imitate it: for I only *imagine* . . . what it must have sounded like to . . . an onlooker. An overseer. Not to *me*; Lord knows! Being *in* it. Or doing it, rather." Only gradually, piece by piece, is the mystery of her fall explained and enlarged. Her plunge into the dark water is the central motif of Albee's verbal patchwork. He expands the significance of her fall—her descent from deck to water, from consciousness to unconsciousness—into an allegory of mortality, loss, and release. The fall becomes as suggestive and flexible an image as the primordial box that frames the two interrelated plays.

In one of her speeches the Long-Winded Lady recalls the time she carried crullers out of a store and saw a horrible accident: death and domesticity, the tragic and the mundane, co-exist in florid juxtaposition. The play is "scored" with many of these leaps between the daily and the timeless, and Albee can get away with them because of his abstract structure; he has allowed himself the freedom available to the non-representational painter.

Albee has set himself up as a conductor, contrasting and blending light tones against dark ones, changing tempo and volume according to his own will. Using the methods of the composer (and of the abstract painter, who needn't worry about his fidelity to nature), Albee has constructed a piece of verbal music, a suite for three voices of vastly different tones. The voice of the Long-Winded Lady, alternately droning and pointed, snappish and mellow, is the one Albee values most, is most comfortable with. Through his dextrous juggling, he has transformed his neurotic, pedestrian matron, a rich widow without purpose or direction, into a symbolic figure in whom the forces of life and death contend for dominance. She becomes the focal link between the everyday world—the world of the crullers—and the infinite, mysterious, palpitating universe that surrounds it. The details of her history are entirely ordinary, and familiar from earlier Albee plays: she has a vicious daughter—a ferocious woman with red nails who thinks of herself as her mother's sexual rival—and the memory of a neat, precise, though not cold husband who suffered a messy and protracted death. Her voice, now lyrical, now whining, now embittered, filled with hatred for her voracious daughter and with respect for her dead husband, is continuous with the elegiac tone of the voice in *Box* (which, near the end, punctuates her own speech). When she was asked by authorities on ship if perhaps her fall might have been a suicide attempt, she told them, "Good heavens, no; *I* have nothing to die for." This final line, recollected in tranquility, is the tonic that resolves the play's contrapuntal tensions; it's the dominant chord that concludes the piece with a trailing whisper. Like all of the playwright's recent work, except *Seascape*, *Box/Mao/Box* suggests that it is All Over.

In *Counting the Ways,* Albee subjects character types familiar from previous plays to further theatrical experiments. A coy, wistful, lost middle-aged couple, He and She, are featured in a series of skits, separated by blackouts, that represent variations on the theme of How Do You Love Me. The characters are banal, perhaps more so here than ever before, and once again Albee tries to transform banality by means of clever theatrical artifice. By placing his standard couple facing the crises of middle-age within a vaudevillian framework, he intends to redeem the ordinariness of their sentiments. What little information we are given about He and She is entirely domestic and small scale—there are no cosmic reverberations here, as in *Box/Mao/Box*. The couple sleep in separate beds; they continually question each other about whether or not they love and are loved; there is much talk about daisies and rose and dandelions (as proofs of love); the wife recalls two boys from her girlhood and reminisces about her high school prom. Her keen sense of order and propriety is revealed in an anecdote she recounts concerning the importance of etiquette: her sister is having a dinner party, and is worried about the seating arrangements of two guests, both of whom are dying, one knowingly, the other not. The story is the most amusing as well as the most tangible element in the play, drawing together Albee's recurrent themes of dying and of the function of order in warding off chaos. Typically, a mundane incident such as who sits where at a dinner is linked to a weighty abstract theme: "I think what my sister has done—unintenionally, I will say, out of great sibling generosity—is: to fashion a test for protocol, so willful that protocol's function as the coding of order will be put into question. Civilization, in other words, will collapse. That is an unsisterly thing to do, an unfriendly one, and it brings up once again all those old questions about veneer."

The play's details, then, are made up of tidbits of domestic realism sprinkled with absurdist motifs, such as He and She's argument about how many children they have. These characters are too slight, too sketchily imagined, to hold our interest in a drama that is played "straight," so Albee tries to conceal their conceptual weakness by surrounding their musings with theatrical razzle-dazzle. He turns this sketch about an estranged middle-aged couple into a coy play of and on words. Lists of words—"Walnuts. Parsley. Bone marrow. Celery root."—and questions ("Do you love me?" is the most frequent)—are repeated with different intonations and rhythms. Albee is delighted by the notion that repetition, in itself, *creates* meaning, as if chanting certain words and phrases throughout the play will lend them magical resonance. The characters often toss the same words back and forth:

HE: Crème Brûlée. What happened to the Crème Brûlée.

SHE: There's no Crème Brûlée.

HE: What do you mean there's no Crème Brûlée?

SHE: There's no Crème Brûlée.

HE: There's *always* Crème Brûlée.

SHE: Not today. Do you love me?

No matter how insistent its repetition, "Crème Brûlée" doesn't acquire special meaning; it doesn't become anything more than a pleasing sound, one of the playwright's favorite foreign words, like the "sedia d'ondalo" that supplies a sound effect in *Box*. These odd words seem more like Albee's indulgence in private pleasure than part of a thematic design: "Crème Brûlée" is a grace note in a play that consists entirely of grace notes.

Scenes are short, separated by blackouts; the attempt is to recreate the clipped, staccato pace of a vaudeville routine. Albee stresses the disparity between the play's skit-like format and its bittersweet revelations the pervasive sense of regret and lost passion that haunts the two stranded characters. At one point, the actors step out of character to talk to the audience, but this tired device of breaking theatrical illusion undermines the heightened theatricality that the play tries to sustain— Albee's juggling act collapses.

In *Counting the Ways,* the author's verbal tics, his shifting rhythms, his repetitions of a limited number of motifs, his deliberate use of pauses and ellipses, replace characterization and narrative to an unprecedented degree. Albee's goal of being a "difficult" writer is here entirely misdirected, since what he offers is only the surface mannerisms (most of which have already hardened into cliche) of experimental theatre, without a seriously worked-out theme to bolster his parade of effects. Albee has nothing substantial to say about this stodgy, cloying couple, and so the play's tricky packaging is simply window-dressing. *Counting the Ways* is clearly designed as an unpopular play; Albee had no intention of presenting it on Broadway, although it was produced, to a severe critical reception, by Britain's National Theatre. But this is "unpopular" theatre of an unrewarding (and, for Albee himself, self-defeating) kind.

Although *Listening* is, in fact, more challenging than *Counting the Ways,* once again manner camouflages a sparse idea. This is Albee's most opaque and convoluted writing so far. Setting, characterization, storyline are deliberately obscure. In this bogus mystery play, a Man, a Woman, and a Girl converge in front of a dry fountain on the grounds of an estate that is now (probably) a mental institution. The Man and Woman may have met there in the past (as guests of the mansion's owner?) when, on the spot where they are now standing, the Woman sexually rejected the Man. Now the Man is a cook at the institution, the Woman (perhaps) is a therapist in charge of a catatonic patient, whom she treats with supreme condescension.

Here, in labored abstraction, is yet another variation on the nuclear Albee family: commanding woman, docile, wounded man, and bitter, violent daughter. The Woman's sneering, teasing treatment of the Man is echoed by her imperious attitude toward her patient. This unholy trio, like other Albee families, is condemned to repeat past patterns; they are chained to their roles. The Woman is forever in command, a virile, vigilant presence who makes merely a show of being sentimental; the Man is in a perpetual fog, forever questioning his "executioner;" the Girl is defiantly disruptive. She is described as a praying mantis—the female of the species bites off the male's head during intercourse.

As in the other chamber plays, Albee underscores the characters' psychological entrapment by repetition of words and phrases. The central leitmotif is the Girl's admonition to the Woman: "You don't listen, pay attention is what I mean." She interjects this archly-phrased sentence throughout, momentarily puncturing the Woman's authoritative manner. The Man says to the Woman: "You're not nice." "Who's nice?" is her inevitable response. Albee thus uses simple words, which are stated and re-stated to create a ceremonial atmosphere; the recurrent exchange between the Man and the Woman becomes a kind of courtship dance, a coy romantic ritual. But repetition does not necessarily heighten drama or uncover meaning. "You're not nice," no matter how many times it is repeated, with no matter how many cunning shifts in tone and inflection, does not carry metaphoric impact.

Throughout the play, actions as well as words are repeated, duplicated. Past and present intertwine. The Woman recites a story about a mysterious girl who long ago accosted her in the park, to show her her bleeding hands. The Girl in the fountain imitates the action as the Woman recalls the past incident, holding up her slit wrists, also as if to gain the Woman's attention and perhaps approval.

As in *Counting the Ways* and *Box/Mao/Box*, details are often curious, seeming to contain some purely private significance and appeal for Albee himself. The dry fountain has a mouse shell (shades of *Tiny Alice?*), a blug egg shell, and a feather. These arcane symbols have no immediate connection to the play. The Girl and the Woman refer obsessively to an event that occurred recently at the institution: the Girl slapped another inmate who had stolen (or borrowed) her blue hand-painted cardboard. Albee dwells on the act of painting the cardboard blue, treating it as though it had great ritualistic significance. "Well, if you want more value from it, from the experience," the Girl explains, "and take *grey* cardboard, mix your colors and paint it, carefully, blue, to the edges, smooth, then it's not *any* blue cardboard but very special: grey cardboard taken and made blue, self-made, self-made blue—better than grey, better than the other blue, because it's self-done. Very valuable, and even looking at it is a theft; touching it, even to take it to a window to see the smooth lovely color, all blue, is a theft. Even the knowledge of it is a theft . . . of sorts." The imagery is entirely private and self-enclosed; Albee's use of "blue" seems merely sentimental and arbitrary because it is not placed in a coherent context.

The history of the girl who gets slapped because she stole the special blue cardboard is recounted in detail. Like the primal Albee mother in *The American Dream*, she too is a child-killer. Deserted by her husband, alienated from the rest of her family, she decided one day that "reality is too *little* for me!" Her extreme isolation reflects that of the Girl in the play, who is similarly alienated from her family and friends and feels abandoned. The Woman contributes her own story of desertion: her grandfather, one day, simply "dispersed," leaving her grandmother, who waited for him for seven years and then went upstairs and took poison.

The play thus recounts events of great violence and passion. The eruptions of torrential feelings all take place off-stage, however, as in Greek tragedy, but unlike Greek tragedy, the *drama* takes place off-stage here as well. Whatever emotions the characters do have is distanced and blurred by the measured cadences of their speech, the remote retrospective tone of their monologues. It's as if the writer himself has become like one of his characters, cling to the ordered pattens of art as a shield against the void. In these late plays, rhythm, repetition, convoluted syntax, "speaking well," are more important than traditional dramatic conflict. These stylized chamber dramas are willfully and needlessly obfuscated.

Some of the writing has the chiseled quality, the poise and lilt, that Albee can always manage, and the longer set speeches are invariably examples of "fine writing." The Woman's story of her grandparents has a sombre, poignant beauty. The off-stage figure of the mad woman who killed her child is intriguing. A few exchanges between the Woman and the Girl catch the distinctive tone of nastiness between women that Albee is famous for. And some of the dialogue between the Woman and the Man recalls the Strindbergian clashes of the early plays. But the three archetypal Albee characters in the play have been submerged beneath a gratuitously opaque style. Speeches, for the most part, do not connect, and we are forced (by design) to listen carefully to discern even the barest sense of context and continuity. The fragmented, cryptic, elliptical language, as if issuing from the characters' unconscious, sounds like private code. Conventional exposition is withheld, or revealed gradually and partially; the impressionistc rendering of character and situation is meant to give the drama an element of the mysterious and the ineffable, but the technique of teasing the audience in this way is by now a cliche of experimental theatre. Neither the characters nor the setting are suggestive enough to support the ceremonial trappings. The tortuous, fractured conversation *is* difficult, but unrewarding because there is no real vision beneath it. The indirectness and preciosity do not express a view of the world, or of the failure of human connection: form does not serve or mirror content; style remains clearly detachible from substance, with the result that *Listening* is a clever, spurious set of exercises, of self-indulgent experiments in line, texture, rhythm.

In *Counting the Ways* and *Listening,* the strict limitations that Albee sets himself—no stories, no fully developed characterizations, the monosyllabic language—are a denial of his virtuosity, his lush sense of language, his harsh satire, his joy in creating explosive, rampaging, exhibitionistic neurotics. Genteel chamber dramas like these two most recent works are really not at all in Albee's line.

IV

Evasions of Sex:
The Closet Dramas

Albee's early one-act, *The Death of Bessie Smith*, blatantly introduces the anti-woman motif that streaks throughout almost all the plays. In this short drama, set, uncharacteristically for Albee, in the South, the nominal social theme of racism is subverted by the writer's obsession with his leading female character. The play has the superficial form of protest drama: the black singer Bessie Smith, whom we never see, dies because she is refused admission to a whites-only hospital. Albee isn't really interested in the race theme, however; the focus of the play is not on Bessie Smith—he is only marginally concerned with the singer's exploitation by an intolerant white society. "Bessie Smith" is simply a convenience, a shorthand method of supplying a dramatic but essentially irrelevant framework for the character he is genuinely interested in, a virulent white nurse—the first monstrous shrew in the canon—who works at the hospital where the legendary singer was denied admission.

The play's action is arranged uncomfortably in a series of interconnected scenes. In the beginning, Albee uses the film technique of cross-cutting to establish parallels between the white and black characters. The link between the separate groups—Jack, Bessie Smith's driver, talking about Bessie's comeback plans; and the Nurse at home and at work—is not disclosed until the climax, when, after a car accident, Jack pleads for Bessie's admission to the hospital, even though he knows that Bessie is already dead.

Representing the intolerance of a Southern white racist point of view, the Nurse is elaborated far beyond her link to the play's social statement. Albee, in fact, does not score her for being a bigot so much as he attacks her for being a castrating female. Her racism is merely a secondary reason for the playwright's scorn. Powerful women hold a fatal fascination for Albee, and he allows this compulsive, voracious, sadistic woman to overtake the play. At the same time that he genuinely despises her, he clearly is delighted with her. Her type releases the full force of his animosity; his scorn, which transforms her into a grotesque parody of female viciousness, reaches surreal dimensions. Albee takes pleasure in watching her unravel, and the play is not about the emblematic death of Bessie Smith but about the progressive breakdown of a supremely ornery, spiteful, terrified, sexually frustrated woman. As a case study of sexual hysteria, the play has terrific energy; but it pales as a dissection and expose' of Southern bigotry.

Albee gleefully provides abundant information—much more than we need to know—about the Nurse's advanced "condition." She is allowed to work out her frustrations on three men: her father, a black orderly, and a handsome white intern. To her father, a semi-invalid, she is openly scornful. "You're nothing but a hanger-on, a flunky," she spits out at him. When she isn't being spiteful, she treats him like a willful, misbehaving child. At the hospital, she baits the high yellow orderly, mocking his self-defeating attempts to be well-behaved, to be "white." "Well . . . you *are* a true little gentleman," she sneers. "You *are* polite . . . and deferential . . . and you are a genuine little ass-licker, if I ever saw one. Tell me, boy . . . is it true that you have Uncle Tom'd yourself right out of the bosom of your family . . . ? Is it true, young man, that you are now an inhabitant of no-man's land, on the one side shunned and disowned by your brethren, and on the other an object of contempt and derision to your betters?. . . . I'll tell you what you do . . . You go north, boy, you go up to New York City, where nobody's any better than anybody else . . . But before you do anything like that, you run on downstairs and get me a pack of cigarettes." With the intern, she plays the castrating mistress, alternately flirtatious and ravenous. "Honey, your neck is in the noose," she growls, "and I have a whip . . . and I'll set the horse from under you . . . when it pleases me." "You will *court* me, boy," she orders, "and you will do it *right!*"

As the play progresses, she is gradually consumed by her rage. The intensity of her anger overwhelms her as well as the play: "I am *sick*. I am sick of everything in this hot, stupid, fly-ridden *world*. I am sick of the disparity between things as they are, and as they should be! I am sick of this desk . . . this uniform . . . it scratches. . . . I am sick of talking to people on the phone in this damn stupid hospital. . . . I am sick of going to bed and I am sick of waking up.

. . . I am tired . . . I am tired of the truth . . . and I am tired of lying about the truth . . . I am tired of my skin. . . . I WANT OUT!"

Although Albee's disproportionate contempt for the character undermines the nominal social thesis, it creates a vivid caricature of female rapacity. The part becomes a showcase for Albee's particular gifts as a writer: his acid wit, his black comedy exaggeration, his delirious bitchiness. And it allows him to work out a grudge against a certain kind of possessive, domineering woman.

The anti-female strain in Albee's work is nakedly obvious. In *The American Dream,* Mommy destroys her son, almost literally gobbling him up. Martha in *Virginia Woolf* is almost a parody of female lachery. The Nurse in *Bessie Smith* is a demon of negative energies. In these early plays, Albee unleashed his misogyny in bitter, hilarious tirades; his intense feelings were expressed in great waves of fierce rhetoric. These wildly funny female gorgons are the most spectacularly written roles in the canon. They are each presented with the kind of theatrical overstatement that is severely chastened in the later chamber plays of more intimate focus. Manic, extroverted, on the warpath, Albee's rampaging women established his reputation.

Mixed with Albee's evident disgust with these women, however, is a kind of complicity, even a certain sly, grudging admiration for their strength, or for their triumph over their weakness. It is too simple to describe Albee as an out-and-out misogynist. In *Seascape,* he creates a wise, relaxed woman, and his matrons in *A Delicate Balance,* in *All Over,* and in *Quotations from Chairman Mao Tse-Tung* are not vicious. They are forbiddingly formal, but they uphold rather than destroy their families. Their commitment to order and decorum provides shelter and necessary, if rather sombre, comfort. Albee clearly intends us to respect them, if not exactly to regard them with warmth. He admires their steadfastness, their stern WASP morality.

The women Albee reserves his sharpest satiric jabs for are the ones who unravel, like the Nurse and Mommy, the hysterics who want everyone to collapse along with them. Women rule the roost in Albee's households; sometimes they govern wisely if icily, sometimes their power is clearly threatening and emasculating. It is significant, though, that women are typically presented as maternal rather than romantic figures.

Sexual fear of powerful women, a theme which is sounded obliquely in almost all the plays, is a major element in two dramas, *Tiny Alice* and *Malcolm*. In these two works, men who are weak enough to be seduced by aggressive women pay with their lives for their moral lapse. In his scathing review of *Tiny Alice*, "The Play That Dare Not Speak Its Name (*The New York Review of Books*, February 25, 1965), Philip Roth accused Albee of writing a disguised homosexual play in which the gay man's fear of sleeping with a woman is presented as an allegory about faith and doubt, appearance and reality:

> Like *Virginia Woolf*, *Tiny Alice* is about the triumph of a strong woman over a weak man. The disaster of the play, however—its tediousness, its pretentiousness, its galling sophistication, its gratuitous and easy symbolizing, its ghastly pansy rhetoric and repartee—all of this can be traced to his own unwillingness or inability to put its real subject at the center of the action. . . . Why *Tiny Alice* is so unconvincing, so remote, so obviously a sham—so much the kind of play that makes you want to rise from your seat and shout, "Baloney"—is that its surface is an attempt to disguise the subject on the one hand, and to falsify its significance on the other. All that talk about illusion and reality

may even be the compulsive chattering of a dramatist who at some level senses that he is trapped in a lie.

Although Roth's harsh reading was attacked at the time as simplistic and reductionist, it is in fact eminently sensible. Roth cuts through the play's topheavy religious and philosophical masquerade to focus on the sexual frustration that is at the core of Albee's fable.

A lay Brother, on an errand for his church, goes to the mansion of Miss Alice, who plans to make a donation of two billion dollars. Brother Julian is unknowingly being used as a scapegoat, since the bequest will be made only if he is sacrificed to the deity Miss Alice represents. In the course of the play, Miss Alice seduces, marries, and then abandons the innocent go-between. Seeing that Julian is really a terrified child, Miss Alice skillfully conceals her sexuality beneath displays of matronly concern. Julian is soothed, caught off-guard. He confesses to Miss Alice that he may once have slept with a woman at the time he was confined to an asylum. His possible lover was a religious hysteric, a woman with delusions that she was the Virgin Mary. Julian himself suffers from an acute Christ complex. He is a masochist, enamored of a voluptuous vision of himself as a martyr. "I have longed . . . to be of great service." he announces to Miss Alice. "When I was young—and very prideful—I was filled with a self-importance that was . . . well disguised. Serve. That was the active word!. . . . I WISH TO SERVE AND . . . BE FORGOTTEN."

For Julian, humiliation and pain are deeply sexual. His fantasy of Christian martyrdom, in which the Romans "used the saints as play-things," produces orgasmic release:

Oh, when I was a child and read of the Romans . . . I could entrance myself, and see the gladiator on me, his trident fork against my neck, and hear, even hear, as much as feel, the prongs as they entered me; the . . . beast's saliva dripping from the yellow teeth, the slack side of the mouth, the . . . sweet, warm breath of the lion; great paws on my spread arms . . . even the rough leather of the pads; and to the point of . . . as the great mouth opened, the breath no longer warm but hot, the fangs on my jaw and forehead, positioned . . . IN. And as the fangs sank in, the great tongue on my cheek and eye, the splitting of the bone, and the *blood* . . . just before the great sound, the coming dark and the silence. I could . . . experience it all. And was . . . engulfed. Oh, martyrdom. To be that. To be able ... to be that.

Julian's notion of martyrdom is a thinly disguised gay fantasy, in which the weak lay Brother is vanquished by a rough gladiator—nelly gay sodomized by butch leather stud.

When Julian gives himself to Miss Alice, it is because of his desire to serve God and Church through the exquisite pleasure of self-sacrifice. Driven by a compulsion to debase himself, enticed by fantasies of physical torture and degradation, Julian makes an excellent patsy, primed for rape. On one level (its lowest), *Tiny Alice* is an overexcited sadomasochistic fantasy, with Julian the willing, quivering masochist to the sadism of the Church. Like the characters in Genet's *The Balcony*, Julian cannot take his sex straight; he can achieve orgasm only through elaborate ceremonies of self-debasement. Sex for him, as for Genet's gamesplayers, must be heavily ritualized.

Albee's methods are as indirect as his character's tortured sexuality. He presents Julian as a man of austere religious scruples who is unable to reconcile an ideal concept of God—God as pure abstraction—with man's limiting, anthropomorphic concept of divinity. Throughout most of the drama, Julian is ravaged by religious doubts, by a crisis of faith. The character's religious confusion—his ache to serve the Church, his struggle to understand the infinite—is, however, only a mask for his sexual hysteria. Between his terror of women and his temperamental inability to be actively homosexual, Julian is sexually traumatized, and Albee has constructed a flamboyant fable in which the scared lay Brother is tricked into heterosexuality.

Julian's "punishment" for sleeping with a woman is extreme: he is betrayed by Miss Alice, by his Cardinal, and by a Lawyer, who is the worldly emissary between Miss Alice and the Church. In the play's allegorical scheme, he is seduced and abandoned by Women, Religion, and Society. And all because he had sex with a woman!

Albee has cleverly elaborated this perverse sexual tale into a multi-focus drama, which is at once a busy religious allegory about one man's loss and recovery of faith; a satire on the worldliness, the corruption, and greed of the Church; a parable about appearance and reality, the symbol and the substance, the abstract and the concrete; a morality play about man's inevitable defeat in reaching for the Platonic Ideal. Since its theatrically charged surface, its overheated drama of religious and philosophical conflict, masks its sexual trauma, the play itself becomes part of the dialectic between appearance and reality that is one of its persistent themes.

As in virtually all of Albee's work, sex is handled evasively, kept at a distance from the play's ostensible focus of dramatic interest. For Julian, the religious and the sexual impulse are hopelessly entangled. Though linked to the character's spiritual quest, sex remains concealed throughout the play. In *Tiny Alice,* the sexual masquerade is more elaborate and more highly charged than in any other Albee drama because the concept of the mask, of subterfuge, is built into the play's method as well as its theme. Everything here is merely a front for something else. Miss Alice is only the earthly representative of the deity Tiny Alice, who is in fact infinite. Miss Alice first confronts Julian in the disguise of an old woman, and, though she takes off this mask, she remains in "costume" for the rest of the play—Julian never does learn exactly who and what she is. Miss Alice, Lawyer, and Butler, the three guardians, are controlled by the mysterious and omnipotent Force of Tiny Alice, and so their behavior is never free or genuine; they're puppets. Inside the mansion is a model of the mansion, and inside that model is another replica. When a fire breaks out in the chapel in the full-scale mansion, there is a facsimile fire in the model, or miniature mansion. Examples of the real and the fake multiply dizzyingly—the play is a mosaic of reflections and replications. Each character and event is therefore seen in symbolic double focus; for Julian, the mansion is a treacherous place because nothing in it is what it seems to be; everything is both smaller and larger than its actual dimensions, thereby hopelessly confounding Julian's romantic quest for the Absolute.

In the fantastic world that the play constructs, then, reality is maddeningly elusive, confusing, hostile. The play itself is confused and confusing, cunning in its slipperiness. Albee, on one level, doesn't want his audience to get it, and his symbolic scaffolding is designed to push us off the track, to keep us away from the central, inescapable theme of the fear of powerful women. The allegorical embellishments keep the sexual neuroses at a distance. (This same kind of self-created aloofnes is evident in Albee's recent mannerist work, where affected language and format build screens against unmanageable feelings.)

Despite the skillful diversionary tactics, *Tiny Alice* contains the ultimate image of enveloping, devouring Womanhood in the canon. The play raises the domineering woman figure that recurs obsessively in Albee's writing to the exalted position of rapacious, all-consuming Deity. Miss Alice, who has been both mother and mistress to Julian, abandons him to the dark powers of the ironically misnamed infinity, Tiny Alice. As he lays dying in the empty mansion, as the force of Tiny Alice overwhelms him, Julian, the abandoned Brother, resembles the many other abandoned, mistreated, fatally maimed children in Albee's work. Like the mutilated child in *The American Dream* and the imaginary child in *Virginia Woolf,* he has been used by his "parents," cruelly manipulated by them for their own self-serving needs. But even in Brother Julian's orgasmic final soliloquy, Albee links the sexual resolution—Tiny Alice overtakes Julian, female force overwhelms male weakness—to the spurious philosophical theme: Julian, we are meant to understand, has been finally united with that Abstraction he has struggled to experience and to visualize: .

> You . . . thou . . . art . . . coming to me?
> ABSTRACTION? . . . ABSTRACTION! . . .
> Art coming to me. How long wilt thou
> forget me, O Lord? Forever? How long wilt
> thou hide thy face from me? . . . Consider

and hear me, O Lord, my God. CONSIDER AND HEAR ME, O LORD, MY GOD. LIGHTEN MY EYES I SLEEP THE SLEEP OF DEATH. BUT I HAVE TRUSTED IN THY MERCY, O LORD. HOW LONG WILT THOU FORGET ME? How long wilt thou hide thy face from me? COME, BRIDE! COME, GOD! COME! Alice? Alice? ALICE? MY GOD, WHY HAST THOU FORSAKEN ME? The bridegroom waits for thee, my Alice . . . is thine. O Lord, my God, I have awaited thee, have served thee in thy . . . ALICE? ALICE? . . . GOD? I accept thee, Alice, for thou art come to me. God, Alice . . . I accept thy will.

At the end, as throughout the play, Albee sets up a network of correspondences: Julian's lust for union with abstraction is both religious and sexual; the language is both mock-sexual (the punning use of "come") and mock-religious (the echoes of Christ's crucifixion); God and Alice are hopelessly enmeshed in Julian's ravings; Julian's martyrdom is equated, in language and iconography, with Christ's. Philip Roth scoffed that Julian's death has "as much to do with Christ's Passion as a little girl's dreaming about being a princess locked in a tower has to do with the fate of Mary Stuart." Julian is likened to Jesus Christ, Roth suggests acidulously, "because he has had to suffer the martyrdom of heterosexual love."

Written in Albee's early, exuberant style, *Tiny Alice* is exciting hocus-pocus. It has enormous theatrical imagination and audacity—it is something of a put-on, a coded gay drama about what happens if you get seduced by a woman. The writing has the verve and attack, the manic energy, evident in the one-acts. The play's opening dialogue between Lawyer and Cardinal, universally admired for its crackling, venomous wit, sets the campy but evasive tone. The exchange between these two poseurs suggests, glancingly, that they were schoolboy lovers. They understand, and are skillfu! in exposing, each other's nastiness:

CARDINAL: What should we do now? Should we clap our hands . . . twice, and have a monk appear? A very old monk?.... And should we send him for wine? Um? Should we offer you wine, and should we send him scurrying off after it? Yes? Is that the scene you expect now?

LAWYER: It's so difficult to know what to expect in a Cardinal's garden, Your Eminence. An old monk would do...or— who is to say? perhaps some good-looking

> young novice, all freshly scrubbed, with
> big working-class hands, who would . . .
>
> CARDINAL: We have both in our service; if
>   a boy is more to your pleasure . . .
>
> LAWYER: I don't drink in the afternoon, so
>   there is need for neither . . . unless Your
>   Eminence . . . ?

The Cardinal wickedly remembers that at
school Lawyer's nickname was Hyena: "Did we
not discover about the hyena that it was a most
resourceful scavenger?" he cackles. "That, fail-
ing all other food, it would dine on offal . . . and
that it devoured the wounded and the dead?
We found that last the most shocking: the
dead. But we were young. And what horrified
us most—and, indeed, what gave us all the
thought that the name was most fitting for
yourself— . . . was that to devour its dead,
scavenged prey, it would often chew into it . . .
chew into it THROUGH THE ANUS????"
Mocking each other's homosexuality, the characters express themselves with campy sarcasm
and irony; their arch, mock-imperial tone
(Cardinal uses "we") has unmistakable elements of stereotypical gay humor. The scene
establishes a connection that runs throughout
the play between the priesthood and homosexuality: "The more urbane of us wondered

about the Fathers at school," Lawyer recalls, "about their vaunted celibacy . . . among one another. Of course, we were at an age when everyone diddled everyone else . . . and I suppose it was natural enough for us to assume that the priests did too." Later, Butler's calling Lawyer "Dear," and his insinuating, flirtatious manner toward Julian underscore the veiled homosexual milieu. In outmoded gay jargon, Tiny Alice is a code term for the anus. Has Albee played a sly in-joke on straight audiences?

Aggressively heterosexual critics like Robert Brustein, Richard Schechner, Philip Roth, and Stanley Kauffmann have accused Ablee of writing closet dramas in which hidden gay motifs sneak by the unsuspecting bourgeois crowd that comprises most of the playwright's audience. Philip Roth summarized the impatience of critics with gay masquerades when he asked, at the end of his review of *Tiny Alice*, "How long before a play is produced on Broadway in which the homosexual hero is presented as homosexual, and not disguised as an angst-ridden priest, or an angry Negro, or an aging actress, or worst of all, Everyman?"

Homosexual imagery and character types are presented indirectly in Albee's plays. One of Albee's many screens as a writer is the one he erects between himself and the subject of homosexuality. Apart from the special case of *Tiny Alice,* only his early plays, *The Zoo Story, The Sandbox,* and *The American Dream,* and his adaptations of the work of other writers, *Malcolm* and *The Ballad of the Sad Cafe,* contain gay motifs, and these are treated circumspectly, almost surreptitiously. Homosexuality is never called by its rightful name, but, as in *Tiny Alice,* is introduced as both something else and something *more* than simple homosexuality. Brother Julian isn't presented as a gay man for whom sleeping with a woman is a fate not worse than but exactly equal to death; he is a tormented seeker after union with a pure, abstract divinity. Similarly, Jerry in *The Zoo Story* doesn't want simply to pick Peter up, he wants to sacrifice himself as a kind of perverse testimonial to human isolation. He is not a cruising gay (Albee hardly confronts this level of the action), he is a haunted, brooding loner with a Christ fixation. Like Brother Julian, Jerry compulsively seeks martyrdom.

Typically, sexual drives in Albee become transfigured into mock-religious acts of sacrifice, penitence, and immolation; sex is incorporated into a lofty symbolic framework. Sex in Albee's work is not a healthy, gusty sport— the happiest celebration of sex in the entire canon is the memory of a long ago summer affair spoken by the Mistress in *All Over* in whick, distanced by time, a teen-age passion is eulogized. Albee's characters customarily use sex either as a deadly weapon in ferocious marital battles, or else abstain from it altogether, like the withered middle-aged couples that figure prominently in the recent plays.

Jerry in *The Zoo Story* is representative of Albee's evasions of sex. The play dramatizes an encounter, on a park bench, between a desperate outsider and a prim family man. Jerry prods and provokes Peter into responding to him; the loner demands attention from the self-contained man he has chosen to communicate with. The confrontation is not presented as specifically homosexual, though gay references are obliquely introduced throughout Jerry's abrasive approaches to Peter. Jerry says that, in his youth, he was homosexual for a week; he makes a crack about cops chasing "queers" out of trees in the park; a colored "queen" lives in one of the cubicles adjoining his in his shabby West Side rooming house. His portrait of his landlady, in whom female desire is presented as malodorous and defiled, is fiercely misogynistic, though certainly not conclusive evidence of the character's being gay. Jerry is unusual in the Albee canon in being an urban wanderer rather than a member of a family, and his isolated city life faintly suggests the behavior of a lonely closet gay, driven compulsively to seek anonymous sexual encounters.

The intensity of Jerry's isolation is outlined in his famous recital of his relationship with a dog. "The Story of Jerry and the Dog" is the first great monologue in a canon particularly rich in the monologue form. Jerry's frantic efforts to get the landlady's dog to notice him— he tries, at one point, to poison the dog— reflect his insistence in reaching Peter. Jerry gladly settles for the dog's hatred, and when the dog finally glares at him, he is relieved, he feels he has been validated: contempt, suspicion, fear, are better than no response at all:

> It's just . . . it's just that . . . it's just that if you can't deal with people, you have to make a start somewhere. WITH ANIMALS! Don't you see? A person has to have some way of dealing with SOMETHING. If not with people . . . if not with people . . . SOMETHING. With a bed, with a cockroach, with a mirror . . . no, that's too hard, that's one of the last steps. With a cockroach, with a . . . carpet, a roll of toilet paper . . . no, not that, either . . . that's a mirror, too. . . . You see how hard it is to find things? With a street

corner, and too many lights, all colors re-
flecting on the oily-wet streets . . . with a
wisp of smoke . . . with pornographic playing
cards . . . with love, with vomiting, with
crying, with fury because the pretty little
ladies aren't pretty little ladies, with making
money with your body which is an act of
love and I could prove it, with howling
because you're alive; with God. How about
that? WITH GOD WHO IS A COLORED
QUEEN WHO WEARS A KIMONO AND
PLUCKS HIS EYEBROWS. . . . Where
better to make a beginning . . . to understand
and just possibly be understood . . . a
beginning of an understanding, than with . .
. . . than with a DOG. Just that; a dog.

Albee presents Jerry's agonizing loneliness
as a universal condition, rather than a specifically gay one. At the end, Jerry impales himself
on a dagger that he has thrust into Peter's
hand. The character's self-willed crucifixion is
intended to give the park bench encounter
allegorical dimensions. The lesson that Jerry
learned at the zoo—the one he keeps threatening to reveal to Peter—is that, like the animals,
we all occupy our separate cages. Jerry im-
molates himself on Peter's knife as a testament
to that dark truth; but on a less exalted level,

does that swift thrust of the dagger suggest sexual penetration as well? "I came unto you," Jerry laughs, faintly, "and you have comforted me. Dear Peter." Sexual climax and crucifixion, as in *Tiny Alice,* are inextricable; death and sexual release mingle in dark alliance.

Homosexual imagery is more blatant, though even less relevant thematically, in *The American Dream* and *The Sandbox.* A bikini-clad young man, a male model type, is a prominent icon in both short pieces. *The American Dream* is a longer version of material first articulated in *The Sandbox*—both plays use the same family consisting of bossy Mommy, namby-pamby Daddy, and acerbic Grandma, and in both the Young Man is an emissary of death, his perfection of form a reminder of mortality. Albee's symbolic use of the beautiful male figure is thus highly charged as well as ambiguous. The body beautiful is placed center stage for the approval of the characters as well as the audience. But the character's physical perfection is associated, as in the work of Tennessee Williams, with death. Albee's Young Man, like Williams's stud figures in play after play, and especially in *The Milk Train Doesn't Stop Here Any More,* is an angel of mercy who guides old women to their end. The Young Man, the American Dream, comes to "call" on Grandma. He treats her with gentleness. He is sensitive and patient, and in some undefined way he is a source of salvation: he represents, for Grandma, an alternative to the confinement and indignity of life in her mean daughter's house. The Young Man himself has a more negative interpretation of his beauty, his physique being merely a shell, a thin cover for emptiness. His external perfection is the objective emblem of the American Dream— the Young Man, who is himself a "dreamboat," is both symptom and result of a national addiction to superficial values; his unblemished form and his supreme passivity, his absence of feeling, indicate a bankrupt national sensibility, a corrupt infatuation with plastic surfaces.

Typically, as a social dramatist, Albee is undistinguished, a mere dabbler in generalizations about false values and deceptive appearances. His use, though, of a curiously de-eroticized hustler-like figure is richly ambiguous. The character is both gentle and vacant, both innocent and cynical. His youth is a reminder of Grandma's age. Albee seems to respond positively to the character's beauty and at the same time to resent him for it, to undermine the beauty as a mask for inner emptiness. Youthful beauty is enshrined as powerful and beckoning, and then attacked for its spiritual vacancy; and so, in ways that remain unresolved and even to some extent unexplored, the American Dream is both admired and satirized, both applauded for his pleasing facade and scored for his festering insides.

Although the Young Man is an image of ripe sexuality, Albee presents him as being sexless. He merely triggers the sexual desires of others. Like the popular notion of the cool hustler, whose Narcissus-like admiration of his own form is self-sufficient, the American Dream does not, cannot, reciprocate. As an icon, the American Dream is a blatantly gay fantasy figure, but Albee avoids presenting the character as specifically gay. The dark world of the sexual outlaw, the urban landscape of John Rechy's *City of Night,* with its compulsive sex-seekers, is only faintly suggested in Albee's play. As a creative writer, Albee is clearly more comfortable in the heterosexual suburban drawing room than in the homosexual underground. Sexual tensions aren't as taut in his work as in Tennessee Williams's, where there is often a conflict between the heterosexual surface and the homosexual undercurrents.

Williams's work often follows the Proustian Albertine strategy, where, because of social pressures, the writer plays it safe by transforming a male figure into a female. Proust transferred his own feelings for a man into a fictional counterpart, who was, for propriety's sake, female. Williams's plays contain the same kind of transference. Hungry women who desire beautiful men are imaginative transformations of the writer's own impulses. There is a deep psychic connection between the playwright, concealing his own sexual identity, and a character like Blanche Du Bois, hiding her sexual rapacity beneath a mask of ladylike gentility. In many ways, Williams benefited from the pressures of social convention, which set limits on what kind of sexuality would be acceptable in the commercial theatre for which he wrote. Williams's sense of restriction creates the explosive sexual tension that bursts through his writing even in his less flavorful later work. Williams is a poet of homosexual longing that is expressed and released through nominally heterosexual characters. The resulting clash between surface image and subtextual resonance has been useful to Williams as a creative artist, if not perhaps always healthy for his psyche. Williams feels, in fact, even after he has publicly come out, in *Memoirs,* and now that it is not only safe but "in" to write an openly gay play, that homosexuality is not a promising subject for him as a dramatist. He fears the results might not have the coiled tensions, the layered quality of the plays that to some extent are masked and coded. Williams thrives on the subterfuge and masquerade that social attitudes have forced on him.

Albee doesn't have Williams's exhibitionistic flair, his great generosity, his openly hungry sexuality. He is a cooler, far more cerebral writer for whom sex is always treated at a distance, usually ironically. Williams celebrates sex, despite that the fact that it can also bedevil his characters; Albee never sees the body as a means of salvation. Albee's writing does not have the tension, demonstrated in Williams's work, of an underground sensibility struggling both to express and to conceal itself within a conventional sexual context. Gay imagery appears around the edges of the frame in several plays, and Albee chooses to keep it there.

Albee is entirely at ease with the tone and the rhythms of the Westchester families whose homes he exposes—he grew up in one. Some critics and audiences, however, have read his continuously hostile and at times almost savage portraits of family life as masked, insidious put-downs of straight ideals, though the notion that fear of overpowering women and pleasure in puncturing the value of family life automatically render a writer's work "homosexual" is wildly prejudicial. In this light, however,

Virginia Woolf has been read as a masked play about two extraordinarily bitchy gay male couples. Straight people don't treat each other like this, with such irony, such rapier wit, such quick repartee, the argument foolishly runs. Heterosexual couples aren't this decadent! Those who see Martha as a man in drag point to the famous opening lines in which she says "What a dump!", thereby parodying the dialogue from a Bette Davis movie. Since Bette Davis has long been a cult figure in the gay world, and since she is one of the favorite targets of female impersonators, doesn't this only underline the play's essentially camp sensibility? Martha's sexuality is thus read as a parody of female desire rather than the thing itself—her interest in sex is mocked, and so she can be seen as an ironic gay projection of what real women are really like. In this interpretation of the play, Martha is the butch gay, Honey is the nelly, and they both conform to gay stereotypes just as much as the campy boys in the band do. And because they are really men in drag, playacting their way through acid portraits of women who are either impossibly domineering or impossibly silly, the two nominally female characters are childless. There are no children in the play because there are no women to produce them! And this is the true explanation for that troublesome imaginary child!

Albee has always dismissed such a reading. He nixed a proposed Broadway revival with males playing Martha and Honey. The camp humor is abundant, certainly, aimed at the knowing but in no way undermining the play for an unsuspecting straight audience. Middle class audiences have laughed at and recognized aspects of themselves in the two ghastly marriages the play dissects, and whatever else they may be, Martha and Honey are convincing as recognizable women, just as much as Blanche or any of Williams's fluttery belles "play" as particular kinds of neurotic females.

Significantly, the plays in which homosexual motifs are most openly treated—*Malcolm* and *The Ballad of the Sad Cafe*—are those adapted from the work of other writers. Like *Tiny Alice, Malcolm* is about the corruption of an innocent. Malcolm is a golden young man, another version of the American Dream, who is ogled by both the male and female characters. Malcolm is also another Albee orphan; he has lost his father in some mysterious way, and he sits, expectantly, on a bench until he is snapped up by Mr. Cox (pun intended), a father surrogate, who becomes his guide and instructor. Mr. Cox, we are told in passing, is a pederast;

and because he is a dirty old man, he sends Malcolm to a series of unsavory people so that the young man may learn more about the world.

Malcolm first visits an old man who is trapped, willingly, in a sadomasochistic marriage. The old gent and his wife— a whore with orange hair—bicker about whether the man is ninety-seven or one-hundred and ninety-two. Malcolm also visits a beatnik artist, who paints his portrait, and her husband, an ex-convict who strokes Malcolm's golden hair and his thigh while protesting, "Look, Malcolm, I'm not a queer or anything, so don't jump like that." But Malcolm's most important visits are to Madame Girard, a voracious rich woman who surrounds herself with beautiful, cackling young men; and to a hot pop singer named Melba, who is accompanied by a punk dressed in leather.

The first act of this mock-morality pageant is dominated by Malcolm's accession to the Girard stable of boys. The second act is given over to Malcolm's marriage to Melba. Melba craves sex and alcohol, and the combination proves fatal to the fragile hero. "Oooooh, you are good at marriage, sweetheart, yes, you are," croons the sodden Melba. "Gimme that mouth of yours, tonguey-boy. Ummmmmmmm. Oh baby let's do marriage right this second sweetheart lover baby dollface, c'mon, C'MON!" Melba treats Malcolm like an idiot child: "Momma got to go work. . . . But you stay right there, sweetheart; you just lie there an' read a funnybook, or somethin', so Momma know where you are when she want you." Castrating mother and twitchy mistress are embodied in a single omnivorous character; and Albee presents Melba's emphatic, overpowering sexuality with contempt. She is a lewd, preposterous character.

Like *Tiny Alice,* the play is bewitched by the notion that sex with demanding women is lethal. The acquistive, super-sophisticated Madame Girard, and the hot to trot Melba— both merciless parodies of female sexuality— promote Malcolm's deterioration. Sex with a nymphomaniac spells his final undoing, his ultimate loss of innocence. Behind the play's mocking treatment of sex is a kind of adolescent terror of normal adult sexuality. Purdy's fable is about the consequences of "doing it" with a woman—sex with Melba coarsens Malcolm, fatally contaminates him.

Albee worked on Purdy's parable of the loss of innocence right after he had completed his own version of the theme in *Tiny Alice.* Purdy's story is much simpler, although the homosexual currents remain as submerged. The play's opening image of blond, ethereal Malcolm seated primly on a golden bench is gay imagery of a particularly romantic and sentimantal kind. But Malcolm never has sex with a man, although it is implied that Mr. Cox "used" him. In his devastating review, Robert Brustein noted the "masked, guarded nature" of the play, concluding that *Malcolm* was (in 1966) Albee's "most deeply homosexual work. As Albee gets closer and closer to his true subjects—the malevolence of women, the psychological impact of Mom, the evolution of the invert—he tends to get more abstract and incoherent until he is finally reduced, as here, to a nervous plucking at broken strings.

But whether gay or straight, sex in the play is presented as distinctly unsavory. All of the marriages—Malcolm's own, as well as the ones he is sent by Mr. Cox to observe—are dramatized as wounding, destructive perversions of human need. Married people are treated with outright contempt.

Malcolm is Albee's most resounding failure. Even his customary verbal deftness falters here. He flattens the spare, cadenced diction of the Purdy novel, and his heavy underlining of the allegorical framework coarsens what is at best a wry cautionary tale for susceptible, handsome young gays.

The Ballad of the Sad Cafe is a more robust treatment of gay characters. Though it is never labeled this exactly, the play concerns a homosexual triangle in which a woman, Amelia, and a man, her former husband Marvin Macy, fight over a midget, Lymon, who has a crush on Marvin. The play is certainly unliberated in its imagery since its lesbian heroine is a big strapping woman who moves like a wrestler, and its homosexual hero is a flirtatious, petulant midget who falls in love with a Marlboro Country fantasy figure.

On her marriage night, Amelia, for reasons never explained, though it is implied that she felt threatened by his potent sexuality, threw Marvin out of her bedroom. A man fiercely proud of his sexual allure, Marvin is humiliated by Amelia's dismissal. He feels shamed in the eyes of the town, and he vows to get even. Years later, Amelia replaces Marvin with her cousin Lymon, who makes no sexual demands on her. The two set up house, their physical differentness—her Amazon size, his dwarfishness—emblematic of their sexual difference. Their communion is invaded by the return of Marvin Macy, the avenging male peacock. For the climax, Amelia and Marvin have a showdown in the public square. Marvin wins, he and Lymon go off together, while Amelia retreats to her house, becoming a recluse who occasionally peers out at the town from behind her shuttered windows.

The rural Southern setting, the characters' countrified diction, the outsider status of the main characters, are all unusual for Albee. This odd sexual fantasy is clearly Carson McCullers's rather than his. McCullers was a bisexual who suffered because of her homeliness and physical illness, and no doubt there was some transference between herself and her character Amelia. But in neither the novella nor in Albee's adaptation is Amelia treated sympathetically. She is a tough woman terrified of showing her vulnerability; for her to be loved is unbearably painful, and she chooses her cousin over Marvin because the midget has no sexual interest in her and because he lacks Marvin's passion. For this frigid woman, Marvin is impossibly threatening.

Through the presence of a narrator, who acts as a screen between the audience and these fantasms of McCullers' sad, lyrical imagination, Albee keeps his distance from the material. Typically, he does not examine the characters' coiled, loaded sexuality. The homosexuality is implicit, as in the novella. Amelia's intense aversion to Marvin's strutting maleness is never explained, never defined as specifically lesbian. Her hatred of male sexuality is palpably rendered, however, and when she and Marvin fight at the end, she seems to be going to battle against all self-regarding studs.

Albee retains the lilting rhythms of McCullers's language, its mellow, nostalgic tone. But these tapestry-like figures, and the strange sexual ritual in which they participate, which develops over a long period of time, are not comfortable on the stage. Seeing their combat enacted in the manner of a Western movie showdown threatens to turn them simply into freaks. The delicacy and poignancy of McCullers's fable cannot really be transferred to a more physical medium. As in *Malcolm,* Albee's literal rendition of symbolic action blunts the original material.

V

Albee at the Crossroads

In its delirious non-sequiturs, its farcical exaggeration of everyday chit-chat, *The American Dream* recalls Ionesco's *The Bald Soprano*. *Who's Afraid of Virginia Woolf?* resembles *Long Day's Journey into Night* in its marathon length, its quartet of bickering characters who strip each other's defenses, its concentrated time span and mounting sense of claustrophobia. *A Delicate Balance* has the cultivated tone of T.S. Eliot's dramas in which prose mingles with and aspires to the rhythms of poetry and in which the daily world is linked to a higher, mysterious realm. The guardians in *Tiny Alice* recall the guardians, also with supernatural associations, in Eliot's

The Cocktail Party. The battle of the sexes in *Virginia Woolf* is Strindbergian in its primal hostilities. The lean, austere prose, the use of recurrent motifs, the non-narrative mode, of *Box/Mao/Box* have strong resemblances to Pinter's *Landscape* and *Silence.* The characters waiting for the end in *All Over* recall Ionesco's metaphoric morality play, *Exit the King,* and more faintly echo Beckett's existential clowns *Waiting for Godot.* The indirectness in the more recent plays, the dramas of the unspoken, recalls Pinter's methods as well as those of Chekhov.

Albee's work thus contains echoes of several great plays and trends of the modern theatre, and yet the accent, the voice, the tone, is finally and unmistakably Albee's own. In cultivating the peculiar rhythms of that voice, in fact, with its fragmented sentences, its repetitions, its starchy epigrams and aphorisms, its arch, haughty syntax and diction, its self-conscious use of colloquialism and cliche, Albee has become a self absorbed stylist, elegant and patrician, rather than a storyteller or a revealer of character. His latest pieces, *Counting the Ways* and *Listening,* impossibly chilly and fussy, are a self-destructive denial of the power so amply manifest in the early work. Albee has misjudged his own talents; his latest plays are undertaken because of an interest in experimenting with a poetic technique, with a new syntax or a more rarefied diction, rather than because he has something to say. Less has not proven more for Albee, as it often has for Pinter; simplifying his language, restricting his theatrical coloring, has produced a series of increasingly arid dramas, wan playlets often expanded unmercifully into a semblance of a full evening's entertainment. In his recent work, Albee has been in search of a form, a style, a pose, rather than a theme. Instead of getting closer to his own experience, drawing on his own biography for the materials of his plays, he seems to be escaping into more and more abstract inquiries into mortality and emptiness. The more sober and cosmic his themes, the less powerful his work has become. Erasing sex from the plays is only the most obvious of Albee's strategies of evasion.

His achievement is nonetheless major. *Virginia Woolf* and *A Delicate Balance* are great modern plays, rich and continuously challenging, and assured of a permanent place in the American repertory. The early one-acts still have energy, especially in performance—they are exhilarating displays of Albee's surging rhetorical power. *Tiny Alice* and *Box/Mao/Box* are the worthy, if finally unsatisfactory, experiments of a born playwright. Their sense of language, and of design, has true daring. The rest of the canon—*All Over*, *Seascape*, *Counting the Ways*, *Listening*, the three adaptations (*Everything in the Garden*, *Malcolm*, *The Ballad of the Sad Cafe*)—are disappointments.

After the dead-end experiments of *Counting the Ways* and *Listening*, the dramatist hopefully will return to writing big, noisy, audacious plays, unafraid to face up to "Virginia Woolf" and to whatever is in Albee himself.

SELECTED BIBLIOGRAPHY

Albee, Edward. *All Over.* New York: Atheneum, 1971.

———. *The American Dream and The Zoo Story.* New York: The New American Library, Signet Books, 1961.

———. *The Ballad of the Sad Cafe.* New York: Atheneum, 1964.

———. *Box and Quotations from Chairman Mao Tse-Tung.* New York: New YorkAtheneum, 1969.

———. *Counting the Ways and Listening.* New York: Atheneum, 1977.

———. *A Delicate Balance.* New York: Atheneum, 1977.

———. *Everything in the Garden.* New York: Atheneum, 1968.

———. *Malcolm.* New York: Atheneum, 1966.

———. *The Sandbox, The Death of Bessie Smith, With Fam and Yam.* New York: The New American Library, Signet Books, 1960.

———. *Seascape.* New York: Atheneum, 1975.

———. *Tiny Alice.* New York: Atheneum, 1965.

———. *Who's Afraid of Virginia Woolf?.* New York: Atheneum, 1964.

Amacher, Richard E. *Edward Albee.* New York: Twayne Publishers, 1969.

Bentley, Eric. *The Life of the Drama.* New York: Atheneum, 1967.

Bigsby, C.W.E., ed. *Edward Albee. A Collection of Critical Essays.* Englewood Cliffs: Prentice-Hall 1975.

Brustein, Robert. *The Third Theatre*. New York: Alfred A. Knopf, 1969.

Debusscher, Gilbert. *Edward Albee: Tradition and Renewal*, trans. Anne D. Williams. Brussels: Center for American Studies, 1969.

Downer, Alan S., ed. *American Drama and its Critics*. Chicago: University of Chicago Press, 1965.

Esslin, Martin. *The Theatre of the Absurd*. New York: Doubleday, Anchor Books, 1961.

Gilman, Richard. *Common and Uncommon Masks*. New York: Random House, 1971.

Ionesco, Eugene. *Notes and Counter Notes*, trans. Donald Watson. New York: Grove Press, 1964.

Paolucci, Anne. *From Tension to Tonic. The Plays of Edward Albee*. Cardondale: Southern Illinois University Press, 1972.

Rutenberg, Michael E. *Edward Albee: Playwright in Protest*. New York: Avon, Discus Books, 1969.

Weales, Gerald. *The Jumping-off Place: American Drama in the 1960's*. New York: Macmillan, 1969.

Willeford, William. "*The Mouse in the Model*," Modern Drama, 12, September 1969, 135-45.

Williams, Tennessee. *Memoirs*. New York: Doubleday, 1975.

Young, Stark. *The Theatre*. New York: Hill and Wang, 1958.

THE AUTHOR

FOSTER HIRSCH is Assistant Professor of English and Film at Brooklyn College. His reviews and articles have appeared in the *New York Times, Chicago Tribune, Harper's Bookletter, Saturday Review, The New Republic, The Nation, The Village Voice, Crawdaddy, Film Quarterly* and *Film Comment.* His other books include profiles of Elizabeth Taylor, Tennessee Williams and Laurence Olivier.